the unusual b

MUSIC TRIVIA

with over 3,500 questions and puzzles

© Brian Whyte 2019

The unusual book of

MUSIC TRIVIA

with over 3,500 questions and puzzles

It is almost forty years since I started in Hospital Radio. My first programme on Grampian Hospital Radio (before moving to Hospital Radio Perth in 2008), was 'Brian Whyte's Conundrum' – a mixture of music and puzzles. It contained posers, such as lyrics and anagrams, along with questions about each record (as it was back then) that was played. I have used some of these original puzzles, and expanded it considerably to produce this work.

This book features puzzles and trivia questions regarding music from the 1950's (and sometimes earlier) up to the present day, so there are plenty of topics for all ages! It contains twenty one different categories (the eagle eyed will notice that each is headed by a song title!), including true or false, anagrams, odd one out, lyrics, real names and filling in the blanks. In some instances the number of spaces indicates the number of letters required. However, in some cases (where it would be too obvious) a continuous dash has been used instead of individual ones.

In general, punctuation marks have been omitted in order to not make the puzzle too obvious, and also there are times when the lead artist is mentioned without the backing group, as that question may crop up in another section. Names of artistes appearing beside a song need not relate to the original, best known, or highest chart placing, of that particular track - but they are associated with the song.

It should be noted that some answers to questions are given that do not relate directly to that category. For example, a song 'June is a great time of year' may be used as a girl's name of 'June' even though it is not intended in that context.

All reference to 'hit' means a chart entry in the UK, unless stated otherwise. It should also be noted that 'the' has often been dropped from a group's name, unless it is an integral part of their title. So, 'The' Beatles are usually referred to as 'Beatles', but no change would be made to 'Mott The Hoople'.

Obviously, music continues to be made, so things are constantly changing. However, all answers were correct at time of going to print.

EMPTY SPACES No.1

Fill in the blanks to reveal musicians who have had chart hits:

1. J_H_ L_N_O_
2. J_H_ K_N_O_
3. D_F_Y
4. J_R_I_ C_C_E_
5. U_T_A _A_E
6. T_M _E_T_
7. L_W_S _A_A_D_
8. A_A_ A_T
9. G_O_I_ G_Y_O_
10. M_R_I_E _C_U_C_E_N
11. F_A_K _I_A_R_
12. M_R_ H_P_I_
13. D_Z_E _A_C_L
14. A_M_N_ V_N _E_D_N
15. C_N_I _A_P_R
16. D_N _A_T_I_G_
17. K_L_E _I_O_U_
18. L_A_Y _E_
19. D_V_D _S_E_
20. G_O_I_ E_T_F_N

EMPTY SPACES No.1

ANSWERS

1. John Lennon.
2. John Kongos
3. Duffy.
4. Jarvis Cocker.
5. Ultra Nate.
6. Tom Petty.
7. Lewis Capaldi.
8. Adam Ant.
9. Gloria Gaynor.
10. Martine McCutcheon.
11. Frank Sinatra.
12. Mary Hopkin.
13. Dizee Rascal.
14. Armand Van Helden.
15. Cyndi Lauper.
16. Don Partridge.
17. Kylie Minogue.
18. Leapy Lee.
19. David Essex.
20. Gloria Estifan.

LUCKY NUMBER No.1

Which cardinal or ordinal numbers are missing from these song titles?

1. _____ coins in the fountain (Frank Sinatra)
2. _____ in the morning (Faron Young)
3. December, _____ (oh, what a night) (Four Seasons)
4. _____ of May (Bee Gees)
5. The _____ and only (Chesney Hawkes)
6. _____ drunken nights (The Dubliners)
7. Goody _____ shoes (Adam Ant).
8. _____ hours from Tulsa (Gene Pitney)
9. _____ sticks (Led Zeppelin).
10. When I'm _____ (The Beatles).
11. _____ bad apple (The Osmonds)
12. Knock _____ times (Dawn)
13. _____ miles high (The Byrds)
14. _____ red balloons (Nena)
15. _____ hand Rose (Barbra Streisand)
16. You're _____ (Ringo Starr)
17. Another _____ bites the dust (Queen).
18. _____ son of a _____ son (Iron Maiden).
19. _____ little boys (Rolf Harris)
20. _____ little birds (Bob Marley).

LUCKY NUMBER No.1

Answers

1   Three.
2   Four.
3   Nineteen sixty three (1963).
4   First.
5   One.
6   Seven.
7   Two.
8   Twenty four.
9   Four.
10 Sixty four.
11 One.
12 Three.
13 Eight.
14 Ninety nine.
15 Second.
16 Sixteen.
17 One.
18 Seventh, seventh.
19 Two.
20 Three.

THE NAME GAME No.1

By what names are the following better known:

1. Reginald Kenneth Dwight.
2. Gordon Matthew Thomas Sumner.
3. Angela Tremble.
4. David Howell Evans.
5. Marshall Bruce Mathers.
6. Marie McDonald McLaughlin Lawrie.
7. John Francis Bongiovi.
8. Anna Georgette Gilford.
9. Paul David Hewson.
10. Richard Starkey.
11. Susan Janet Ballion.
12. Georgios Kyriacos Panayiotou.
13. Gaynor Hopkins.
14. Jiles Perry Richardson.
15. Mary Isabel Catherine Bernadette O'Brien.
16. Thomas John Woodward.
17. Stefani Joanne Angelina Germanotta.
18. Christopher John Miller.
19. Curtis James Jackson.
20. Sheena Shirley Orr.

THE NAME GAME No.1

Answers

1. Elton John.
2. Sting.
3. Debbie Harry.
4. The Edge.
5. Eminem.
6. Lulu.
7. John Bon Jovi.
8. Honey G.
9. Bono.
10. Ringo Starr.
11 Siouxsie Sioux.
12. George Michael.
13. Bonnie Tyler.
14. The Big Bopper.
15. Dusty Springfield.
16. Tom Jones.
17. Lady Gaga.
18. Rat Scabies.
19. 50 Cent.
20. Sheena Easton.

MIX IT UP No.1

Can you unravel the anagrams to identify these hit making bands?

1. LAMER ADAM
2. CUE A BLONDE
3. BARREN CRIES
4. WEE AL SHELTERS
5. CARMEN NERO
6. SO STRESS CRISIS
7. INLAND FIRES
8. RARE ROSE STAFF
9. RIOT SHAME
10. LAKE HARK US
11. CAB
12. SECRET MANCHESTER PAIR
13. WET FILES
14. NOW I FOUL UP TRUST
15. LEG IS CRISP
16. LEADS
17. LOUD BY SOME
18. LONGER TONSILS
19. REAL NET
20. LET OSTRICH GET CLEAR

MIX IT UP No.1

Answers

1. MARMALADE
2. DEACON BLUE
3. CRANBERRIES
4. STEALERS WHEEL
5. AMEN CORNER
6. SCISSOR SISTERS
7. LINDISFARNE
8. TEARS FOR FEARS
9. AEROSMITH
10. KULA SHAKER
11. ABC
12. MANIC STREET PREACHERS
13. WESTLIFE
14. UNIT FOUR PLUS TWO
15. SPICE GIRLS
16. SLADE
17. MOODY BLUES
18. ROLLING STONES
19. ETERNAL
20. ELECTRIC LIGHT ORCHESTRA

BLANK SPACE No.1

Fill in the blanks to reveal bands that have had chart hits:

1. A _ T _ C   _ A _ E _ A
2. U _ I _   F _ U _   P _ U _   T _ O
3. V _ S _ G _
4. W _ L _   T _ E   _ O _ N
5. E _ E _ T _ I _   L _ G _ T   _ R _ H _ S _ R _
6. U _ B _ N   _ O _ K _ E   _ O _ L _ C _ I _ E
7. B _ O _ S _ I   _ E _ T
8. A _ E _   C _ R _ E _
9. C _ E _ N   _ A _ D _ T
10. S _ O _   P _ T _ O _
11. M _ N _ R _ D   _ A _ N
12. W _ I _ E _ N _ K _
13. S   _ L _ B _
14. J _ T _ R _   T _ L _
15. D _ E _   P _ R _ L _
16. T _ K _   T _ A _
17. A _ L   _ A _ N _ S
18. S _ U _ H _ I _ E   _ P _ N _ E _ S
19. B _ C _ M _ N   _ U _ N _ R   _ V _ R _ R _ V _
20. A _ E   _ F   _ A _ E

BLANK SPACE No.1

ANSWERS

1. Aztec Camera.
2. Unit Four Plus Two.
3. Visage.
4. Walk The Moon.
5. Electric Light Orchestra.
6. Urban Cookie Collective.
7. Bronski Beat.
8. Amen Corner.
9. Clean Bandit.
10. Snow Patrol.
11. Manfred Mann.
12. Whitesnake.
13. S Club 7.
14. Jethro Tull.
15. Deep Purple.
16. Take That.
17. All Saints.
18. Southside Spinners.
19. Bachman Turner Overdrive.
20. Ace of Base.

COMMON PEOPLE No.1

What do the following have in common?

1. Eric Haydock, Terry Sylvester, Carl Wayne, Graham Nash, Bernie Calvert.

2. The power of love, Move closer, I'm your man, Frankie, Easy lover.

3. Michael Ball, New Seekers, Bonnie Tyler, Matt Monro, Black Lace.

4. Isn't it a wonder, Key to my life, Father and son, Love is a hurricane, You needed me.

5. Steve Hackett, Chris Stewart, Peter Gabriel, Ray Wilson, Anthony Phillips.

6. Exile on Main Street, Goat's head soup, Aftermath, Voodoo Lounge, Tattoo you.

7. The Joker, Take the money and run, Abracadabra, Rocki'n me, Fly like an eagle.

8. Heartbreaker, Grease, Chain reaction, Guilty, Evening star.

9. David Crosby, Gene Parsons, Michael Clarke, Roger McGuinn, Clarence White.

10. Glockenspiel, mandolin, bass guitar, reed and pipe, grand piano.

11. Junior Campbell, Mark Knopfler, Donovan, Jim Diamond, Lonnie Donegan.

12. True confessions, Deep sea skiving, Pop life, Please yourself, Wow!

13. A flock of seagulls, The Christians, Dead or alive, Frankie goes to Hollywood, The Farm.

14. Ruth Ann, Ed Drewett, Emeli Sande, Maverick Sabre, Lily Allen.

15. Picture this, Maria, Atomic, Union City blue, Sunday girl.

16. Paul Jones, Mike Vickers, Jack Bruce, Klaus Voorman, Mike D'Abo.

17. Little white bull, Consider yourself, Living doll, From Russia with love, Rock with the caveman.

18. The great escape, 13, Leisure, Think tank, The magic whip.

15. Price tag, Grenade, Glad you came, Loca people, Read all about it.

20. Alexandra Burke, Little Mix, Shayne Ward, Matt Cardle, Leona Lewis.

COMMON PEOPLE No.1

ANSWERS

1. They have all been members of The Hollies.
2. They were all No.1's of 1985.
3. They have all represented the UK in the Eurovision Song Contest.
4. They are all Boyzone singles.
5. They have all been members of Genesis.
6. They are all albums by the Rolling Stones.
7. They are all singles by the Steve Miller Band.
8. They were all written (or co-written) by Barry Gibb.
9. They were all members of the Byrds.
10. They were all instruments introduced by Viv Stanshall on Mike Oldfield's iconic album 'Tubular Bells'.
11. They were all born in Glasgow.
12. They are all Bananarama albums.
13. They all originated from Liverpool.
14. They have all had hits with Professor Green.
15. They were all hit singles by Blondie.
16. They were all members of Manfred Mann.
17. They were all written by Lionel Bart.
18. They are all albums by Blur.
19. They were all No.1 hits from 2011.
20. They were all winners of The X Factor.

WORDS No.1

Can you identify these famous songs from their opening lyrics:

1. I met a gin-soaked, bar-room queen in Memphis ...

2. Slip inside the eye of your mind, don't you know you might find ....

3. I got chills. They're multiplying, and I'm losing control ....

4. I'd sit alone and watch your light, my only friend through teenage nights .....

5. There's a fire starting in my heart, reaching a fever pitch ....

6. Deep down in Louisiana close to New Orleans. Way back up in the woods ....

7. I never meant to cause you any sorrow. I never meant to cause you any pain ...

8. Smile, an everlasting smile. A smile could bring you near to me .....

9. The warden threw a party in the county jail. The prison band was there. and they began to wail ....

10. Do you feel like a chain store? Practically floored. One of many zeros ....

11. You saw me standing by the wall corner of a main street, and the lights are flashing on your window sill ....

12. I'm dancing on the White House lawn, sipping tea by the Taj Mahal at dawn ....

13. You, you're such a big star to me. You're everything I wanna be .....

14. When you're weary, feeling small. When tears are in your eyes, I will dry them all ....

15. Welcome to your life. There's no turning back. Even while we sleep, we will find ...

16. As I walk along I wonder, a-what went wrong with our love. A love that was so strong ......

17. The club isn't the best place to find a lover, so the bar is where I go .....

18. Don't think I can't feel that there's something wrong. You've been the sweetest part of my life for so long ....

19. The sirens are screaming and the fires are howling way down in the valley tonight ....

20. She was more like a beauty queen from a movie scene. I said I don't mind, but what do you mean ....

WORDS No.1

Answers

1. Honky tonk women (Rolling Stones)

2. Don't look back in anger (Oasis)

3. You're the one that I want (John Travolta and Olivia Newton John)

4. Radio Gaga (Queen).

5. Rolling in the deep (Adele).

6. Johnny B. Goode (Chuck Berry).

7. Purple rain (Prince).

8. Words (Bee Gees).

9. Jailhouse rock (Elvis Presley).

10. Coffee and TV (Blur).

11. Save a prayer (Duran Duran).

12. Life is a minestrone (10CC).

13. Shine (Take That).

14. Bridge over troubled water (Simon and Garfunkel).

15. Everybody wants to rule the world (Tears for Fears).

16. Runaway (Del Shannon).

17. Shape of you (Ed Sheeran).

18. Think twice (Celine Dion).

19. Bat out of Hell (Meatloaf).

20. Billie Jean (Michael Jac

TWO OF US No.1

Can you complete the names of these duos?

1. Simon and ?
2. Paul and Barry ?
3. Althea and ?
4. Donny and Marie ?
5. Zager and ?
6. Windsor Davies and ?
7. Daphne and ?
8. Mack and Katie ?
9. Peter and ?
10. Peaches and?
11. Godley and ?
12. Jon and ?
13. Phatts and ?
14. Sonny and ?
15. Ashford and ?
16. Esther and Abi ?
17. Sam and ?
18. Captain and ?
19. Nina and ?
20. Ike and Tina ?

TWO OF US No.1

Answers

1. Garfunkel.
2. Ryan.
3. Donna.
4. Osmond .
5. Evans.
6. Don Estelle.
7. Celeste.
8. Kissoon.
9. Gordon.
10. Herb.
11. Creme.
12. Vangelis.
13. Small.
14. Cher.
15. Simpson.
16. Ofarim.
17. Dave.
18. Tennille.
19. Frederick.
20. Turner.

WHO ARE YOU? No.1

Which name is missing from these song titles?

1   I can't let _ _ _ _ _ _ go (Honeybus)

2   _ _ _ _ _ _ _ _ (Marillion)

3   _ _ _ _ _ _ Jones (The Supremes)

4   See _ _ _ _ _ play (Pink Floyd)

5   Happy _ _ _ _ (The Who)

6   Dear _ _ _ _ _ _ _ _ (Souixsie Souix)

7   _ _ _ _ _ _ _ (Tom Jones)

8   _ _ _ le Taxi (Vanessa Paradis)

9   _ _ _ _ _ (Barry Manilow)

10   _ _ _ _ _ don't be a hero (Paper Lace)

11   _ _ _ _ _ _ (Elton John)

12   Long tall _ _ _ _ _ (Little Richard)

13   _ _ _ _ _ _ (Dolly Parton)

14   _ _ _ _ _ _ _ Rigby (The Beatles)

15   Proud _ _ _ _ (Tina Turner)

16   _ _ _ _ _ (Paul Anka)

17   Oh _ _ _ _ _ _ _ _ (Shaggy)

18   The _ _ _ _ genie (David Bowie)

19   _ _ _ _ _ _ _, it was really nothing (The Smiths)

20   _ _ _ _ _ _ _ Brown (The Coasters)

WHO ARE YOU? No.1

Answers

1. Maggie.
2. Kayleigh.
3. Nathan.
4. Emily.
5. Jack.
6. Prudence.
7. Delilah.
8. Joe.
9. Mandy.
10. Billy.
11. Daniel ... or ... Nikita.
12. Sally.
13. Jolene.
14. Eleanor.
15. Mary.
16. Diana.
17. Carolina.
18. Jean.
19. William.
20. Charlie.

WOULD I LIE TO YOU? No.1

Are the following statements true or false?

1. Celine Dion won the Eurovision Song Contest in 1988 singing for Switzerland.

2. The Queen albums 'A night at the opera' and 'A day at the races' are also the titles of two Marx Brothers films.

3. 'Come on you reds' was a UK No.1 hit in 1994 for Liverpool FC.

4. Nobel Prize winner, physicist Max Plank, was the grandfather of Olivia Newton-John.

5. Elvis Presley was the first singer to record 'Hound Dog'.

6. 'Dave Dee and the New Yorkers' was the original name of Dave Dee, Dozy, Beaky, Mick and Tich.

7. 'With a little help from my friends' was originally recorded by the Beatles on Sgt Pepper's Lonely Hearts Club Band.

8. 'Fox' was the name shared by a British band and an Australian band of the 1970's.

9. 'Club Tropicana' was the first Top Ten hit for Wham!

10. In 1999, Will Smith released an album called 'Willenium'.

11. Ronnie Carroll is the only person who has represented the UK at the Eurovision Song Contest two years in a row.

12. The duo Alisha's Attic were the daughters of singer Brian Poole.

13. Katie Black and Julie De Martino were known as 'The Ting Tings'.

14. Guys and Dolls singer Julie Forsyth was the daughter of entertainer Bruce Forsyth.

15. Del Amitri's only Top Ten hit was 'Nothing ever happens'.

16. The Bluebells No.1 'Young at heart' was originally recorded by Bananarama

17. Ronnie Wood has had hits with The Move, ELO and Wizzard.

18. 'We've got the whole world in our hands' was a hit for Nottingham Forrest with Black Lace.

19. Brothers Fred and Richard Fairbrass were known as 'Right Said Fred'.

20. Brandon Flowers was lead singer with The Killers.

WOULD I LIE TO YOU? No.1

Answers

1. True.
2. True.
3. False - it was by Manchester United.
4. False - it was Nobel Prize winner, physicist Max Born .
5. False - it was Willie Mae 'Big Mama' Thornton, who recorded it in 1952. It was her biggest hit.
6. False - it was Dave Dee and the Bostons.
7. True.
8. True.
9. False. It was their fourth. The first was 'Young Guns (go for it)'.
10. True.
11. True - and achieved fourth place on both occasions.
12. True - Shelly and Karen.
13. False - it's Katie White and Jules De Martino.
14. True.
15. False - they never had a Top Ten hit. Nothing ever happens peaked at No.11..
16. True - it featured on their album 'Deep sea skiving'.
17. False - it was Roy Wood.
18. False - it was with Paper Lace.
19. True.
20. True.

EMPTY SPACES No.2

Fill in the blanks to reveal musicians who have had chart hits:

1. A _ E _ A _ D _ R _ N _ A _
2. R _ B _ I _ W _ L _ I _ M _
3. N _ I _ D _ A _ O _ D
4. J _ M _ I _ M _ N _
5. J _ S _ G _ N _ A _ E _
6. N _ T _ L _ E _ M _ R _ G _ I _
7. B _ N _ Y _ H _ L _
8. A _ V _ N _ T _ R _ U _ T
9. E _ E _ I _ A _ D _
10. E _ G _ E _ E _ T _ U _ P _ R _ I _ K
11. S _ N _ I _ H _ M
12. C _ I _ P _ A _ S _ P _ T _ R _
13. P _ T _ R _ N _ R _
14. J _ S _ G _ Y _ N _
15. S _ N _ A _ O _ O _ N _ R
16. D _ S O _ O _ N _ R
17. T _ S _ I _ A _ C _ E _
18. C _ E _ N _ Y _ A _ K _ S
19. E _ M _ B _ N _ O _
20. S _ M _ O _ K _

EMPTY SPACES No.2

ANSWERS

1. Alexander O'Neal.
2. Robbie Williams.
3. Neil Diamond.
4. Jim Diamond.
5. Jose Gonzalez.
6. Natalie Imbruglia.
7. Benny Hill.
8. Alvin Stardust.
9. Emeli Sande.
10. Englebert Humperdink.
11. Sandi Thom.
12. Crispian St Peters.
13. Peter Andre.
14. Jess Glynne.
15. Sinead O'Connor.
16. Des O'Connor.
17. Tasmin Archer.
18. Chesney Hawkes.
19. Emma Bunton.
20. Sam Cooke.

JOIN TOGETHER No.1

These groups were known for backing which musician?

1. The Heartbreakers.
2. The Shadows.
3. The Revolution.
4. The Dakotas.
5. The Pacemakers.
6. Showdown.
7. The Miracles.
8. His Comets.
9. The Waves.
10. The Muffins.
11. The Jaywalkers.
12. The Pips.
13. The News.
14. The Teenagers.
15. The Gladiators.
16. The Sunshine Band.
17. The Range.
18. The Union Gap.
19. The Delrons.
20. The Radio Revellers.

JOIN TOGETHER No.1

Answers

1. Tom Petty.
2. Cliff Richard.
3. Prince.
4. Billy J Kramer.
5. Gerry (Marsden).
6. Gary Lee.
7. Smokey Robinson.
8. Bill Haley.
9. Katrina (Leskanich).
10. Martha (Ladly).
11. Peter Jay.
12. Gladys Knight.
13. Huey Lewis.
14. Frankie Lymon.
15. Nero.
16. KC.
17. Bruce Hornsby.
18. Gary Puckett.
19. Reparata.
20. Anthony Steel.

THE NAME GAME No.2

By what names are the following better known:

1. Richard Wayne Penniman.
2. LaDonna Adrian Gaines.
3. Raymond Ian Burns.
4. Richard Graham Sarstedt.
5. Stevland Hardaway Judkins.
6. Reginald Leonard Smith.
7. William James Adams.
8. Susan Traynor.
9. Paul David Hewson.
10. Noel Scott Engel.
11. Christopher John Davidson.
12. Michael Scheuer.
13. Katheryn Elizabeth Hudson.
14. Florencia Bicenta de Casillas-Martinez Cardona.
15. Booker Taliaferro Jones.
16. Concetta Rosa Maria Franconero.
17. Stuart Leslie Goddard.
18. Anthony Fitzgerald.
19. Sean John Combs.
20. Dino Paul Crocetti.

THE NAME GAME No.2

Answers

1. Little Richard.
2. Donna Summer.
3. Captain Sensible.
4. Eden Kane.
5. Stevie Wonder.
6. Marty Wilde.
7. Will.i.am.
8. Noosha Fox.
9. Bono.
10. Scott Walker.
11 Chris de Burgh.
12. Mike Sarne.
13. Katie Perry.
14. Vikki Carr.
15. Booker T.
16. Connie Francis.
17. Adam Ant.
18. Tony Christie.
19. Puff Daddy.
20. Dean Martin.

ALL SHOOK UP No.1

Can you unravel the anagrams to identify these music personalities?

1. LESLEY VIPERS
2. FBI SLAM TOY
3. TONY POLLARD
4. MAP OF AI HALT
5. ANDY BLOB
6. I PROBE SEXIST HELLO
7. TEN MOJOS
8. CLEAN BY OIL
9. JENNYS LEGS
10. MARYS A BAND
11. STALL OF BEANS
12. PRESBYTERIANS
13. BOLT PARTNER
14. DO MOVE TAIL
15. IS AT ROOM
16. FILED DOE MILK
17. LOSE YEAR
18. PILOT EXIT
19. I LAY SKI ACE
20. LIKLEY MARE

ALL SHOOK UP No.1

Answers

1. ELVIS PRESLEY
2. FAT BOY SLIM
3. DOLLY PARTON
4. PALOMA FAITH
5. BOB DYLAN
6. SOPHIE ELLIS-BEXTOR
7. TOM JONES
8. BILLY OCEAN
9. JESS GLYNNE
10. BRYAN ADAMS
11. FONTELLA BASS
12. BRITNEY SPEARS
13. ROBERT PLANT
14. DEMI LOVATO
15. TORI AMOS
16. MIKE OLDFIELD
17. LEO SAYER
18. PIXIE LOTT
19. ALICIA KEYS
20. KELLY MARIE

HAPPY BIRTHDAY No.1

Can you identify these musicians?

1. Singer born in Miami, USA on 1 July 1945.
2. Guitarist born in Newcastle upon Tyne, England on 28 October 1941.
3. Singer born in Bradford, England on 12 July 1984.
4. Singer born in Glasgow, Scotland on 29 April 1931.
5. Drummer born in London, England on 13 September 1965.
6. Singer born in Bangor, Wales on 23 June 1984
7. Bassist born in Bournemouth, England on 21 November 1968..
8. Drummer born in Dundalk, Ireland on 17 March 1973.
9. Singer born in Hoboken, USA on 12 December 1915.
10. Singer born in Halifax, England on 17 February 1991.
11. Drummer born in Birmingham, England on 27 January 1944.
12. Singer born in Frankston, Australia on 13 May 1954.
13. Saxophonist born in Preston, England on 9 March 1963.
14. Singer born in Cambridge, England on 26 September 1948.
15. Singer born in Perth Amboy, USA on 2 March 1962.
16. Guitarist born in Richmond upon Thames, England on 19 July 1947.
17. Singer born in London, Canada on 1 March 1994.
18. Singer born in Liverpool, England on 13 February 1971.
19. Singer born in Witham, England on 14 May 1984.
20. Guitarist born in Lincoln, USA on 5 October 1978.

HAPPY BIRTHDAY No.1

Answers

1. Debbie Harry.
2. Hank Marvin.
3. Gareth Gates.
4. Lonnie Donegan.
5. Zak Starkey.
6. Duffy.
7. Alex James.
8. Caroline Corr.
9. Frank Sinatra.
10. Ed Sheerin.
11. Nick Mason.
12. Johnny Logan.
13. Ian Kirkham.
14. Olivia Newton-John.
15. John Bon Jovi.
16. Brian May.
17. Justin Bieber.
18. Sonia (Evans).
19. Olly Murs.
20. James Valentine.

BLANK SPACE No.2

Fill in the blanks to reveal bands that have had chart hits:

1. S _ I _ E   _ I _ L _
2. D _ E _   B _ U _   S _ M _ T _ I _ G
3. S _ U _ E _ E
4. N _ W   _ I _ S   _ N   _ H _   B _ O _ K
5. 4   _ O _   B _ O _ D _ S
6. S _ A _ L   _ A _ E _
7. T _ L _ I _ G   _ E _ D _
8. D _ V _   D _ E   _ O _ Y   _ E _ K _   M _ C _   A _ D   _ I _ H
9. L _ R _   R _ C _ I _ G _ A _ S   _ I
10. B _ D _ I _ G _ R
11. C _ L _ U _ E   _ L _ B
12. B _ O _ D _ E
13. L _ M _   B _ Z _ I _
14. S _ M _ L _   M _ N _ S
15. G _ A _ L _   B _ R _ L _ Y
16. H _ E   _ N _   C _ Y
17. H _ M _ L _   P _ E
18. C _ S _ A _ A
19. N _ Z _ R _ T _
20. H _ R _ E _   H _ U _ E _   _ A _ D

BLANK SPACE No.2

ANSWERS

1. Spice Girls.
2. Deep Blue Something.
3. Squeeze.
4. New Kids on the Block.
5. 4 Non Blondes.
6. Small Faces.
7. Talking Heads.
8. Dave Dee, Dozy, Beaky, Mick and Tich.
9. Lord Rockingham's XI.
10. Badfinger.
11. Culture Club.
12. Blondie.
13. Limp Bizkit.
14. Simple Minds.
15. Gnarls Barkley.
16. Hue and Cry.
17. Humble Pie.
18. Cascada.
19. Nazareth.
20. Hermes House Band.

WORDS No.2

Can you identify these famous songs from their opening lyrics:

1. A long, long time ago. I can still remember how that music used to make me smile ...

2. I wake up with bloodshot eyes. Struggle to memorise the way it felt ....

3. Try to see it my way. Do I have to keep on talking till I can't go on? ....

4. Libraries gave us power, then work came and made us free .....

5. Close your eyes, give me your hand, darling. Do you feel my heart beating? ....

6. Me with the floorshow, kickin' with your torso. Boys getting high ....

7. Where it began, I can't begin to knowin'. But then I know it's growing strong ...

8. When I was young, my father said 'Son, I've got something to say' .....

9. I made it through the wilderness, somehow I made it through. Didn't know how lost I was ....

10. I can almost see it. That dream I'm dreaming. There's a voice inside my head ....

11. White chalk written on red brick. Our love, told in a heart ....

12. What's wrong with the world, Mama. People livin' like they ain't got no mamas ....

13. Sometimes I feel I've got to run away, I've got to get away from the pain .....

14. You need coolin', baby I'm not foolin'. I'm gonna send you back to schoolin' ....

15. Don't start me talking. I could talk all night. My mind goes sleepwalking ...

16. Where do I begin? Should I tell you how bad I need you now? You're underneath my skin ......

17. Wouldn't it be nice to get on with me neighbours. But, they make it very clear they've got no room for ravers .....

18. If this world is wearing thin and you're thinking of escape. I'll go anywhere with you ....

19. When I was just a little girl, I asked my mother what will I be? Will I be pretty? ....

20. We've been broken down to the lowest turn. Bein' on the bottom line sure ain't no fun ....

WORDS No.2

Answers

1. American Pie (Don McLean).

2. Makes me wonder (Maroon 5).

3. We can work it out (The Beatles).

4. A design for life (Manic Street Preachers).

5. Eternal Flame (The Bangles).

6. Rock DJ (Robbie Williams).

7. Sweet Caroline (Neil Diamond).

8. Bachelor boy (Cliff Richard).

9. Like a virgin (Madonna).

10. The climb (Miley Cyrus).

11. Jennifer Eccles (The Hollies).

12. Where is the love? (Black Eyed Peas).

13. Tainted love (Soft Cell).

14. Whole lotta love (Led Zeppelin).

15. Oliver's army (Elvis Costello).

16. Please don't let me go (Olly Murs).

17. Lazy Sunday (Small Faces).

18. Stay (Shakespears Sister).

19. Whatever will be will be - Que sera sera (Doris Day).

20. The only way is up (Yazz).

THERE'S A PLACE No.1

Which place name is missing from these song titles?

1   Back in the _ _ _ _   (The Beatles)

2   _ _ _ _ _ in your hand   (T'Pau)

3   All the way to _ _ _ _ _ _ _   (Mott the Hoople)

4   _ _ _ _ _ _ _ _ _ Lou   (The Scaffold)

5   _ _ _ _ _ _ calling   (The Clash)

6   _ _ _ _ _ _   (David Essex)

7   _ _ _ _ _ _ _ _ Garden   (Siouxsie Sioux).

8   In _ _ _ _ _   (Johnny Wakelin).

9   _ _ _ _ _ _ _   (Boney M).

10 Born in the _ _ _   (Bruce Springsteen).

11 Midnight in _ _ _ _ _ _   (Kenny Ball)

12 Night boat to _ _ _ _ _   (Madness)

13 _ _ _ _ _ _ _ _ _ _ girls   (Beach Boys)

14 _ _ _ _ _ _ _ _   (Beautiful South)

15 _ _ _ _ _ _ _ _ _ _ _ freedom   (Elton John)

16 Banks of the _ _ _ _   (Olivia Newton John)

17 Don't cry for me _ _ _ _ _ _ _ _ _   (Julie Covington).

18 The poor people of _ _ _ _ _   (Winifred Atwell).

19 Midnight train to _ _ _ _ _ _ _   (Gladys Knight).

20 Cold _ _ _ _ _ _   (Plastic Ono Band).

THERE'S A PLACE No.1

Answers

1	USSR.
2	China.
3	Memphis.
4	Liverpool.
5	London.
6	Tahiti.
7	Hong Kong.
8	Zaire.
9	Belfast.
10	USA.
11	Moscow.
12	Cairo.
13	California.
14	Rotterdam.
15	Philadelphia.
16	Ohio.
17	Argentina.
18	Paris.
19	Georgia.
20	Turkey.

YOU'RE THE ONE No.1

Can you spot the odd one out in each case?

1   Hey Jude, Something, All you need is love, Lady Madonna, Penny Lane.

2   Modern life is rubbish, The great escape, Leisure, Dig out your soul, The magic whip.

3   Japanese Boy, Under pressure, The reflex, Ghost town, Stand and deliver.

4   Revelations, Angels and demons, It's a mystery, Thunder in the mountains, War boys.

5   Hold my girl, Breakaway, Over the creek, Listen to the man, Blame it on me.

6   Union of the snake, My own way, Rio, Save a prayer, Hungry like the wolf.

7   John Entwhistle, Roger Daltrey, Keith Moon, Paul Rodgers, Pete Townshend.

8   Stay beautiful, Profit in peace, Little baby nothing, The everlasting, Indian summer.

9   Denny Doherty, Maddy Prior, Michelle Phillips, Jill Gibson, John Phillips.

10 Graham Gouldman, Paul Hancox, Eric Stewart, Lenny Davidson, Ric Rothwell.

11 Radio Ga Ga, I want to be free, Body language, Hammer to fall, I want it all.

12 Shirley Bassey, James Bradfield, Cerys Matthews, Tom Jones, Richard Ashcroft.

13 Make you feel my love, Rolling in the deep, Skyfall, Someone like you, Chasing pavements.

14 Ring ring, Love and kisses, Arrival, The visitors, Voulez-vous.

15 Give a little love, Uptown top ranking, Wuthering Heights, Summer nights, Rivers of Babylon.

16 Steve Marker, Simon Fowler, Andy Bennett, Oscar Harrison, Damon Minchella.

17. X&Y, Ghost Stories, Mylo Xyloto, Parachutes, Eyes Open.

18 Dollar, Carpenters, The Communards, Culture Club, Pet shop Boys.

19 Wishing I was there, Big mistake, Word is out, Wrong impression, Smoke.

20 Old golden throat, Eyes that see in the dark, Star portrait, Itchy feet, Everybody loves a nut.

YOU'RE THE ONE No.1

Answers

1. Something - was written by George Harrison. The others by Lennon / McCartney.

2. Dig out your soul - is an Oasis album. The others are by Blur.

3. The reflex - was a No.1 hit in 1984, the others topped the chart in 1981.

4. Thunder in the mountains - all the others were on the EP 'Four from Toyah'.

5. Hold my girl - is from George Ezra's 'Staying at Tamara's', the others are from 'Wanted on voyage'.

6. Union of the snake - is from Duran Duran's 'Seven and the ragged tiger', the others are taken from 'Rio'.

7. Paul Rodgers - was with Free, Bad Company, Queen etc, the rest were with the Who.

8. Profit in peace - is by Ocean Colour Scene, the rest were by Manic Street Preachers.

9. Maddy Prior - was with Steeleye Span, the others were The Mamas and Papas.

10. Lenny Davidson - was a member of the Dave Clark 5, the rest were the Mindbenders.

11. I want to be free - was released by Toyah, all the rest were by Queen. 'I want to break free' was a hit for Queen.

12. Richard Ashcroft - is English, all the others are Welsh.

13. Make you feel my love - was written by Bob Dylan, the others were co-written by Adele.

14. Love and kisses - is an album by Brotherhood of Man, the others are by Abba

15. Give a little love - was No.1 in 1975, the others topped the chart in 1977.

16. Steve Marker - was in Garbage, the others were with Ocean Colour Scene.

17. Eyes Open - is an album by Snow Patrol, the others are by Coldplay.

18. Culture Club - was a four piece band, the others are duos.

19. Word is out - was a single by Kylie Minogue, the others are by Natalie Imbruglia.

20. Eyes that see in the dark - is an album by Kenny Rogers, the others are albums by Johnny Cash.

WHO ARE YOU? No.2

Which name is missing from these song titles?

1   _ _ _ _ _ (Dean Friedman)
2   Sexy _ _ _ _ _ (The Beatles)
3   _ _ _ _ _ _ where's your troosers (Andy Stewart)
4   Dear _ _ _ _ _ _ (Madonna)
5   _ _ _ _ _ _ hill (Coldplay)
6   _ _ _ _ _ _ (Cliff Richard)
7   I'd rather _ _ _ _ (Reynolds Girls)
8   Nice guy _ _ _ _ _ (Sleeper)
9   _ _ _ _ _ _ _ III (Supergrass)
10   L - L - _ _ _ _ (Mud)
11   _ _ _ _ _ gun (The Clash)
12   St. _ _ _ _ _ _ _ of the roses (Malcolm Vaughan)
13   _ _ _ _ _ _ 's theme (best that you can do) (Christopher Cross)
14   _ _ _ _ _ (Cuff Links)
15   Worried about _ _ _ (Hoosiers)
16   _ _ _ _ 's prayer (Danny Wilson)
17   _ _ _ _ _ in the shell (Howard Jones)
18   Dear _ _ _ _ _ (Roy Wood)
19   The ballad of _ _ _ _ _ Pumpkin (XTC)
20   _ _ _ _ was here (Candy Dulfer)

WHO ARE YOU? No.2

Answers

1	Lydia ..... or Ariel.
2	Sadie.
3	Donald.
4	Jessie.
5	Violet.
6	Carrie.
7	Jack.
8	Eddie.
9	Richard.
10	Lucy.
11	Tommy.
12	Therese.
13	Arthur.
14	Tracy.
15	Ray.
16	Mary.
17	Pearl.
18	Elaine.
19	Peter.
20	Lily.

EMPTY SPACES No.3

Fill in the blanks to reveal musicians who have had chart hits:

1.   P _ _   P _ O _ Y
2.   R _ C _ E _   P _ A _ T _ N
3.   A _   G _ E _ N
4.   J _ S _ I _   B _ E _ E _
5.   K _ K _   D _ E
6.   O _ I _   R _ D _ I _ G
7.   J _ N _   L _ W _ E
8.   F _ T   _ O _   S _ I _
9.   C _ R _   D _ U _ L _ S
10.   D _ M _   L _ V _ T _
11.   J _ H _ N _   W _ K _ L _ N
12.   G _ E _ O _ Y _   _ O _ T _ R
13.   C _ E _ Y _   C _ L _
14.   P _ A _ T _ C _   _ E _ T _ A _ D
15.   G _ O _ G _   H _ R _ I _ O _
16.   F _ N _ E _ L _   B _ S _
17.   L _ N _   L _ V _ C _
18.   B _ Y _ N   _ D _ M _
19.   M _ X _   _ Y _ R _ V _ S
20.   V _ N _ S _ A   _ A _ A _ I _

EMPTY SPACES No.3

ANSWERS

1. P J Proby.
2. Rachel Platten.
3. Al Green.
4. Justin Bieber.
5. Kiki Dee.
6. Otis Redding.
7. Jona Lewie.
8. Fat Boy Slim.
9. Carl Douglas.
10. Demi Lovato.
11. Johnny Wakelin.
12. Gregory Porter.
13. Cheryl Cole.
14. Plastic Bertrand.
15. George Harrison.
16. Fontella Bass.
17. Lene Lovich.
18. Bryan Adams.
19. Max Bygraves.
20. Vanessa Paradis.

THE FIRST No.1

1. What was the title of Blondie's first UK No.1 hit single?
2. Which group's debut album was called 'Piper at the gates of dawn'?
3. What is the first track on the Beatles' 'Abbey Road'?
4. 'Do what U like' was the first single released by which group?
5. Whose debut album, and first No.1 hit was called 'The Fame'?
6. What was the title of the first Top 10 hit single by Blur?
7. 'Please please me' was the first album by which group?
8. Which recording was the first release on the Virgin label?
9. 'In the flesh?' is the first track on which Pink Floyd album?
10. What was the title of Cliff Richard's first No.1 hit single?
11. 'Wannabe' was the first hit single for which group?
12. 'So far away' was the first track on which Dire Straits album?
13. What was the title of the first Top 10 hit single by Pulp?
14. Which group was first to see their first three singles all reach No.1?
15. What was Neil Diamond's first (and biggest) UK hit?
16. 'Funny funny' was the first hit for which group?
17. Who was the original keyboard player with the Small Faces?
18. What was the first hit single by Amy Winehouse?
19. 'Kissing to be clever' was which band's first album?
20. 'Hello' is the first track on which Oasis album?

THE FIRST No.1

Answers

1. Heart of glass.
2. Pink Floyd.
3. Come together.
4. Take That.
5. Lady Gaga.
6. There's no other way.
7. The Beatles.
8. Tubular Bells by Mike Oldfield.
9. The Wall.
10. Living doll.
11. Spice Girls.
12. Brothers in arms.
13. Common people - in 1994, twelve years after their first single release!
14. Gerry and the Pacemakers.
15. Cracklin' Rosie.
16. The Sweet (four years after their first single release!).
17. Jimmy Winston.
18. Stronger than me.
19. Culture Club.
20. (What's the story) Morning glory?

ANY COLOUR YOU LIKE No.1

Which colour is missing from these song titles?

1. _____ tambourine (Lemon Pipers)
2. Long cool woman in a _____ dress (The Hollies)
3. Fade to _____ (Visage)
4. _____ is the colour (Chelsea FC)
5. Frozen _____ juice (Peter Sarstedt)
6. _____ Cadillac (Prince)
7. _____ river (Creedence Clearwater Revival).
8. Golden _____ (Stranglers).
9. _____ night (Deep Purple).
10. Mellow _____ (Donovan).
11. _____ wedding (Billy Idol)
12. 99 _____ balloons (Nena)
13. Tie a _____ ribbon (Dawn)
14. _____ , _____ grass of home (Tom Jones)
15. Old _____ shoe (The Beatles)
16. _____ (U2)
17. The lady in _____ (Chris de Burgh).
18. Mr _____ sky (Electric Light Orchestra)
19. Nights in _____ satin (Moody Blues).
20. _____ Betty (Ram Jam).

ANY COLOUR YOU LIKE No.1

Answers

1   Green.
2   Black.
3   Gray.
4   Blue.
5   Orange.
6   Pink.
7   Green.
8   Brown.
9   Black.
10 Yellow.
11 White.
12 Red.
13 Yellow.
14 Green, green.
15 Brown.
16 Scarlet.
17 Red.
18 Blue.
19 White.
20 Black.

THE NAME GAME No.3

By what names are the following better known:

1. Adam Richard Wiles.
2. Rita Maria Crudgington.
3. Orville Richard Burrell.
4. Sandra Ann Goodrich.
5. Michael Holbrook Penniman.
6. William Howard Ashton.
7. Onika Tanya Maraj.
8. Roberta Lee Streeter.
9. Shawn Corey Carter.
10. Graham Pulleyblank.
11. James Newell Osterberg.
12. Eilleen Regina Edwards.
13. Joseph Saddler.
14. David Albert Cook.
15. Robyn Fenty.
16. Walden Robert Cassotto.
17. Dylan Kwabena Mills.
18. Ellen Naomi Cohen.
19. James Michael Aloysius Bradford.
20. Terence Nelhams-Wright.

THE NAME GAME No.3

Answers

1. Calvin Harris.
2. Cheryl Baker.
3. Shaggy.
4. Sandie Shaw.
5. Mika.
6. Billy J Kramer.
7. Nicki Minaj.
8. Bobbie Gentry.
9. Jay-Z.
10. Leapy Lee.
11 Iggy Pop.
12. Shania Twain.
13. Grandmaster Flash.
14. David Essex.
15. Rihanna (and that's her middle name - that we left out!).
16. Bobby Darin.
17. Dizzee Rascal.
18. Mama Cass Elliot.
19. Jimmy Nail.
20. Adam Faith.

MIX IT UP No.2

Can you unravel the anagrams to identify these hit making bands?

1. SALLY CUTS PODS
2. PURE MESS
3. CHOP IT I CRY
4. OH RAF CORD
5. DEATH ROOM
6. TICK INTO MEAT
7. SPIN CLIP
8. BAT FOR UPPERS
9. GIVE AS
10. END WITH A BRAVE AGE
11. VAIN RAN
12. IF SHE FORGOT
13. FIVER A LOAF
14. GRASS TAZER
15. LIONS PREP ME
16. NO LOW PARTS
17. MISTER MARSH HEN
18. WED BITCH *
19. VIP NOON SO FULL
20. KATH TATE

MIX IT UP No.2

Answers

1. PUSSYCAT DOLLS
2. SUPREMES
3. CHICORY TIP
4. ROACHFORD
5. MOTORHEAD
6. ATOMIC KITTEN
7. LIPPS INC
8. PREFAB SPROUT
9. VISAGE
10. AVERAGE WHITE BAND
11. NIRVANA
12. FOO FIGHTERS
13. LOVE AFFAIR
14. STARGAZERS
15. LEMON PIPERS
16. SNOW PATROL
17. HERMAN'S HERMITS
18. B*WITCHED
19. LOVIN' SPOONFUL
20. TAKE THAT

BLANK SPACE No.3

Fill in the blanks to reveal bands that have had chart hits:

1. A _ U _
2. R _ X _   M _ S _ C
3. S _ O _ E   _ O _ E _
4. D _ T _ O _ T   _ M _ R _ L _ S
5. D _ T _ O _ T   _ P _ N _ E _ S
6. S _ I _ G   _ U _   S _ S _ E _
7. B _ A _ K   _ A _ B _ T _
8. H _ A _ T
9. J _ C _ S _ N   _ I _ E
10. B _ A _ T _ F _ L   _ O _ T _
11. L _ N _ R _   S _ Y _ Y _ D
12. S _ O _ T _ N _   F _ R   _ I _ L _
13. C _ A _ R _ E _   O _   T _ E   _ O _ R _
14. R _ X _ T _ E
15. B _ F _ Y   _ L _ R _
16. C _ P _ A _ N   _ N _   T _ N _ I _ L _
17. S _ A _ U _   Q _ O
18. M _ R _ L _ I _ N
19. E _ A _ E _ C _ N _ E
20. L _ N _ I _ F _ R _ E

BLANK SPACE No.3

ANSWERS

1. Aqua.
2. Roxy Music.
3. Stone Roses.
4. Detroit Emeralds.
5. Detroit Spinners.
6. Swing Out Sister.
7. Black Sabbath.
8. Heart.
9. Jackson Five.
10. Beautiful South.
11. Lynyrd Skynyrd.
12. Scouting For Girls.
13. Chairmen of the Board.
14. Roxette.
15. Biffy Clyro.
16. Captsin and Tennille.
17. Status Quo.
18. Marillion.
19. Evanescence.
20. Lindisfarne.

WE ARE FAMILY No.1

Which human relations are missing from these song titles?

1   _ _ _ of a preacher man (Dusty Springfield)

2   I saw _ _ _ _ _ kissing Santa Claus (Beverley Sisters)

3   _ _ _ _ _ _ Norman (Marmalade)

4   _ _ _ _ _ _ friction (Haysi Fantayzee)

5   He ain't heavy, he's my _ _ _ _ _ _ _ (The Hollies)

6   _ _ _ _ _ _ nature's _ _ _ (The Beatles)

7   Lock up your _ _ _ _ _ _ _ _ _ (Slade)

8   _ _ _ _ _ _ Jane (New World)

9   My _ _ _ _ _ _ 's eyes (Eric Clapton)

10 _ _ _ _ (Dave Berry)

11 The _ _ _ of Hickory Holler's tramp (O C Smith)

12 Like _ _ _ _ _ _ and _ _ _ _ _ _ (The Drifters)

13 _ _ _ _ _ _ _ (Clive Dunn)

14 Your _ _ _ _ _ _ should know (The Beatles)

15 Footballer's _ _ _ _ (Amy Macdonald)

16 Annie, I'm not your _ _ _ _ _ (Kid Creole)

17 The _ _ _ _ _ _ we share (Chvrches)

18 There's no one quite like _ _ _ _ _ _ (St Winifred's School Choir)

19 My _ _ _ _ _ _ _ Jake (Free)

20 Big bad _ _ _ _ (Foxy Brown featuring Dru Hill).

WE ARE FAMILY No.1

Answers

1	Son.
2	Mommy.
3	Cousin.
4	Sister.
5	Brother.
6	Mother, son.
7	Daughters.
8	Sister.
9	Father.
10	Mama.
11	Son.
12	Sister, brother.
13	Grandad.
14	Mother.
15	Wife.
16	Daddy.
17	Mother.
18	Grandma.
19	Brother.
20	Mama.

WORDS No.3

Can you identify these famous songs from their opening lyrics:

1. See the stone set in your eyes. See the thorn twist in your side. I'll wait for you ...

2. When you left me all alone at the record hop, you told me you were going out for a soda pop ....

3. Never let it be said, that romance is dead. 'Cause there's so little else occupying my head ....

4. I met a devil woman, she took my heart away. She said, I've had it comin' to me .....

5. The silicon chip inside her head gets switched to overload ....

6. Friday night I'm going nowhere, all the lights are changing green to red ....

7. Such a feelin's comin' over me. there is wonder in most everything I see ...

8. I want to hold 'em like they do in Texas, please. Fold 'em, let 'em, hit me .....

9. (Turn around) Every now and then I get a little bit lonely....

10. Standing in the dock at Southampton, trying to get to Holland or France ....

11. She's into superstitions, black cats and voodoo dolls. I feel a premonition ....

12. I blame you for the moonlit sky, and the dream that died with the eagle's flight ....

13. I've never seen you looking so lovely as you did tonight .....

14. Don't worry about a thing, 'cause every little thing gonna be alright ....

15. You talk like Marlene Dietrich, and you dance like Zizi Jeanmaire ...

16. Anyone who ever held you would tell you the way I'm feeling ......

17. You could hear the hoof beats pound as they raced across the ground .....

18. We, we don't have to worry 'bout nothing, 'cause we got the fire ....

19. No New Year's Day to celebrate. No chocolate covered candy hearts to give away ....

20. They say that you're a runaround lover, but you say it isn't so ....

WORDS No.3

Answers

1. With or without you (U2).

2. Lipstick on your collar (Connie Francis).

3. Ruby (Kaiser Chiefs).

4. You ain't seen nothing yet (Bachman Turner Overdrive).

5. I don't like Mondays (Boomtown Rats).

6. Babylon (David Gray).

7. Top of the world (The Carpenters).

8. Poker face (Lady Gaga).

9. Total eclipse of the heart (Bonnie Tyler).

10. The ballad of John and Yoko (The Beatles).

11. Livin' la vida loca (Ricky Martin).

12. Sleeping satellite (Tasmin Archer).

13. The lady in red (Chris de Burgh).

14. Three little birds (Bob Marley).

15. Where do you go to my lovely? (Peter Sarstedt).

16. Stars (Simply Red).

17. Ernie (the fastest milkman in the west) (Benny Hill).

18. Burn (Ellie Goulding).

19. I just called to say I love you (Stevie Wonder).

20. The night has a thousand eyes (Bobby Vee).

LIVIN' THING No.1

Which creatures are missing from these song titles?

1. Hound _ _ _ (Elvis Presley)
2. Three little _ _ _ _ _ (Bob Marley)
3. _ _ _ _ train (Frankie Laine)
4. When _ _ _ _ _ cry (Prince)
5. Rocky _ _ _ _ _ _ (The Beatles)
6. _ _ _ people (putting out fire) (David Bowie)
7. _ _ _ _ _ in the grass (Dave Dee, Dozy, Beaky, Mick and Tich)
8. _ _ _ _ _ _ _ gals (Malcolm McLaren)
9. I'm a _ _ _ _ _ (Lulu)
10. Funky _ _ _ _ _ _ (Goodies)
11. _ _ _ _ _ _ _ (Everly Brothers)
12. Theme from the _ _ _ _ hunter (Cavatina) (The Shadows)
13. Magic _ _ _ (Space)
14. Hungry like the _ _ _ _ (Duran Duran)
15. _ _ _ eat _ _ _ (Adam Ant)
16. Tie me _ _ _ _ _ _ _ _ down, sport (Rolf Harris)
17. El _ _ _ _ _ _ pasa (Simon and Garfunkel)
18. _ _ _ _ _ _ spanner (Dave and Ansell Collins)
19. Madam _ _ _ _ _ _ _ _ _ (Un bel di vedremo) (Malcolm McLaren)
20. _ _ _ _ _ _ _ 's garden (The Beatles).

LIVIN' THING No.1

Answers

1	Dog.
2	Birds.
3	Mule.
4	Doves.
5	Racoon.
6	Cat.
7	Snake.
8	Buffalo.
9	Tiger.
10	Gibbon.
11	Bird dog.
12	Deer.
13	Fly.
14	Wolf.
15	Dog, dog.
16	Kangaroo.
17	Condor.
18	Monkey.
19	Butterfly.
20	Octopus.

WHO ARE YOU? No.3

Which name is missing from these song titles?

1   _ _ _ _ _ _ (Kool & the Gang)

2   _ _ _ _ _ _ _ _ (Overlanders)

3   Bad, bad _ _ _ _ _ Brown (Jim Croce)

4   _ _ _ _ _ (Blondie)

5   _ _ _ _ _ _ _ _ Juniper (Donovan)

6   Oh! _ _ _ _ _ (Neil Sedaka)

7   _ _ _ _ _ (Lewis Capaldi)

8   _ _ _ _ don't take your love to town (Kenny Rogers)

9   _ _ _ _ _ (John Travolta)

10 _ _ _ _ _ _ _, _ _ _ _ _ _ and _ _ _ _ (Marvin Gaye)

11 Cotton-eyed _ _ _ (Rednex)

12 _ _ _ _ _ _ _ beware of the devil (Dandy Livingstone)

13 Lovely _ _ _ _ (Beatles)

14 _ _ _ _ _ _ and the jets (Elton John)

15 Desperate _ _ _ (Lieutenant Pigeon)

16 _ _ _ _ _ _ _ _ _ _ _ (Beach Boys)

17 Pictures of _ _ _ _ (Who)

18 _ _ _ _ _ _ (Sister Sledge)

19 A message to you, _ _ _ _ (Specials)

20 Polk salad _ _ _ _ _ (Elvis Presley)

WHO ARE YOU? No.3

Answers

1. Joanna.
2. Michelle.
3. Leroy.
4. Maria ..... or Denis.
5. Jennifer.
6. Carol.
7. Grace.
8. Ruby.
9. Sandy.
10. Abraham, Martin, John.
11. Joe.
12. Suzanne.
13. Rita.
14. Bennie (sometimes labelled 'Benny').
15. Dan.
16. Barbara Anne.
17. Lily.
18. Frankie.
19. Rudy.
20. Annie.

ALL SHOOK UP No.2

Can you unravel the anagrams to identify these music personalities?

1. LINE ON DICE
2. HIS NEPAL HERO
3. EVIL RAN ME
4. RED DONG LAW
5. ALL TRUE PACK
6. OIL LEVEL COSTS
7. AVERY NESTS
8. I LIKE ME ON GUY
9. CLONED MAN
10. RASH TURNS LOVED
11. CHAIRS FORTH CARD
12. ANY RAT CAN SIN
13. AHA MAD FIT
14. MY LIONS CAR
15. LOIS UPMAN
16. REGAL BY JIM
17. I REGAL QUEEN ISIS
18. A LONG GRIT DROP
19. ALL DAY IN SWIM
20. ERIC SANK DIVA

ALL SHOOK UP No.2

Answers

1. CELINE DION
2. HELEN SHAPIRO
3. LEE MARVIN (Musician? Well, he did have a No.1 hit!)
4. ANDREW GOLD
5. PETULA CLARK
6. ELVIS COSTELLO
7. RAY STEVENS
8. KYLIE MINOGUE
9. DON McLEAN
10. LUTHER VANDROSS
11. RICHARD ASHCROFT
12. NANCY SINATRA
13. ADAM FAITH
14. CARLY SIMON
15. PAUL SIMON
16. MARY J BLIGE
17. ENRIQUE IGLESIAS
18. GORDON GILTRAP
19. ANDY WILLIAMS
20. DIANA VICKERS

EMPTY SPACES No.4

Fill in the blanks to reveal musicians who have had chart hits:

1. J _ S _ I _   J
2. S _ A _ T _   S _ N _ W _ C _
3. L _ N _ Y   _ R _ V _ T _
4. T _ R _ Y   _ A _ K _
5. R _ T _   O _ A
6. F _ R _   K _ N _ E _
7. T _ M _ Y   _ T _ E _ E
8. S _ A _   K _ N _ S _ O _
9. S _ Z _   Q _ A _ R _
10. P _ U _ O   _ U _ I _ I
11. M _ N _ I _   R _ P _ R _ O _
12. K _ N _ E   _ E _ T
13. N _ K   _ E _ S _ A _
14. C _ A _ A   _ H _ N
15. R   _ E _ L _
16. R _ D   _ T _ W _ R _
17. C _ N _ I   _ T _ T _ N
18. S _ O _ M   _ U _ E _
19. E _ L _ E   _ O _ L _ I _ G
20. R _ Y   _ H _ R _ E _

EMPTY SPACES No.4

ANSWERS

1. Jessie J.
2. Scanty Sandwich.
3. Lenny Kravitz.
4. Terry Jacks.
5. Rita Ora.
6. Fern Kinney.
7. Tommy Steele.
8. Sean Kingston.
9. Suzi Quatro.
10. Paulo Nutini.
11. Minnie Riperton.
12. Kanye West.
13. Nik Kershaw.
14. Chaka Khan.
15. R Kelly.
16. Rod Stewart.
17. Candi Staton.
18. Storm Queen.
19. Ellie Goulding.
20. Ray Charles.

HAPPY BIRTHDAY No.2

Can you identify these musicians?

1. Singer born in Auckland, New Zealand on 3 December 1979.
2. DJ born in Dumfries, Scotland on 17 January 1984.
3. Singer born in Conisbrough, England on 25 April 1943.
4. Singer born in Dun Laoghaire, Ireland on 5 October 1951.
5. Guitarist born in Wallington, England on 24 June 1944.
6. Singer born in Port of Spain, Trinidad and Tobago on 8 December 1982.
7. Singer born in Banff, Scotland on 11 August 1981.
8   Rapper born in London, England on 27 November 1983.
9. Singer born in Sydney, Australia on 7 February 1975.
10 Singer born in Douglas, Isle of Man on 22 December 1949.
11. Guitarist and vocalist born in Ystrad Mynach, Wales on 2 August 1948.
12. Singer born in Barnwell, USA on 3 May 1933.
13. Singer born in Sheffield, England on 19 September 1963.
14. Keyboard player born in Johannesburg, South Africa on 21 October 1940.
15. Singer born in Liverpool, England on 18 June 1940.
16. Singer born in Albuquerque, USA on 20 August 1992.
17. Singer born in Dublin, Ireland on 18 January 1983.
18 Singer born in Lennoxtown, Scotland on 3 November 1948.
19. DJ born in Amstelveen, Netherlands on 14 May 1996.
20. Singer born in Belfast, Northern Ireland on 31 August 1945.

HAPPY BIRTHDAY No.2

Answers

1. Daniel Bedingfield.
2. Calvin Harris.
3. Tony Christie.
4. Bob Geldof.
5. Jeff Beck.
6. Nicki Minaj.
7. Sandi Thom.
8. Professor Green.
9. Natalie Imbruglia.
10. Robin Gibb ..... as was Maurice Gibb also!
11. Andy Fairweather Low.
12. James Brown.
13. Jarvis Cocker.
14. Manfred Mann.
15. Paul McCartney.
16. Demi Lovato.
17. Samantha Mumba.
18. Lulu.
19. Martin Garrix.
20. Van Morrison.

LUCKY NUMBER No.2

Which cardinal or ordinal numbers are missing from these song titles?

1   (Call me) Number _____ (Tremeloes)

2   _____ (Prince)

3   _____ days a week (The Beatles)

4   Rainy day women # _____ and _____ (Bob Dylan)

5   _____ ways to leave your lover (Paul Simon)

6   _____ minutes to midnight (Iron Maiden)

7   Route _____ (Chuck Berry)

8   _____ to _____ (Dolly Parton)

9   ' _____ (Queen)

10 _____ nervous breakdown (Rolling Stones).

11 Cloud _____ (Temptations)

12 _____ years (David Bowie)

13 _____ - _____ - _____ (Len Barry)

14 _____ seas of rhye (Queen)

15 It takes _____ (Marvin Gaye and Kim Weston)

16 # _____ dream (John Lennon)

17 _____ psalms (Robert Plant).

18 Revolution _____ (The Beatles)

19 _____ mile high city (Ocean Colour Scene)

20 _____ and _____ is _____ (Medicine Head)

LUCKY NUMBER No.2

Answers

1   One.
2   Nineteen ninety nine (1999).
3   Eight.
4   Twelve, thirty five.
5   Fifty.
6   Two.
7   Sixty six.
8   Nine, five.
9   Thirty nine.
10 Nineteenth.
11 Nine.
12 Five.
13 One, two, three.
14 Seven.
15 Two.
16 Nine.
17 Twenty nine.
18 One ..... or Nine.
19 One hundred.
20 One, one, one.

THERE'S A PLACE No.2

Which place name is missing from these song titles?

1   _____ (Pussycat)

2   _____ ___ (Bobby Bloom)

3   Let's go to ___ _____ (Flowerpot Men)

4   24 hours from _____ (Gene Pitney)

5   A windmill in old _____ (Ronnie Hilton)

6   _____ (Perry Como)

7   Walking in _____ (Cher)

8   _____ town (UB40)

9   _____ swings (Roger Miller)

10   (Is this the way to) _____ (Tony Christie)

11   Do you know the way to ___ ____ (Dionne Warwick)

12   _____ gap (Lonnie Donegan)

13   Witch queen of ___ _____ (Redbone)

14   Woman from _____ (Deep Purple)

15   Viva ___ _____ (Elvis Presley)

16   ____ boat song (Roger Whittaker and Des O'Connor)

17   _____ lineman (Glen Campbell).

18   ___ ____ mining disaster 1941 (Bee Gees).

19   The _____ song (Alan Price).

20   Going to _____ (Led Zeppelin).

THERE'S A PLACE No.2

Answers

1	Mississippi.
2	Montego Bay.
3	San Francisco.
4	Tulsa.
5	Amsterdam.
6	Delaware.
7	Memphis.
8	Kingston.
9	England.
10	Amarillo.
11	San Jose.
12	Cumberland.
13	New Orleans.
14	Tokyo.
15	Las Vegas.
16	Skye.
17	Wichita.
18	New York.
19	Jarrow.
20	California.

WOULD I LIE TO YOU? No.2

Are the following statements true or false?

1. Deep Purple was formed in Hertford in 1968.

2. Jack and Meg White of the duo White Stripes were a married couple.

3. The Jethro Tull album 'Thick as a brick' was written by eight year old genius, Gerald Bostock.

4. Elton John originally intended recording 'Don't go breaking my heart' with Dusty Springfield and not Kiki Dee.

5. 'The Mugwumps' split up to form the 'Lovin' Spoonful' and 'The Mamas and Papas'.

6. At over seven minutes, 'Hey Jude' by the Beatles is the longest record to reach No.1.

7. All sixteen albums released by the group Darts had 'darts' in the title.

8. Barbara Dickson was born in Alnwick, Northumberland.

9. Led Zeppelin was originally called 'New Yardbirds'.

10. At nine years old, Little Jimmy Osmond is the young solo act to top the UK charts.

11. Christine McVie was lead singer with Blue Mink before joining Fleetwood Mac.

12. The Fugees were previously known as Tranzlator Crew.

13. Steve Harley was born as Stephen Nice.

14. Peter Andre was born in Limassol, Cyprus.

15. Lananeeneenoonoon was a group consisting of Kathy Burke, Dawn French and Jennifer Saunders.

16. Kevin Parrott and Michael Coleman had a No.1 hit in 1978

17. 'Dark side of the moon' is Pink Floyd's biggest selling album.

18. Dani Filth and George Ezra were both born in Hereford.

19. Jak Airport and Lora Logic were members of 'X-Ray Spex'.

20. Andy Kim, Leonard Cohen and Bryan Adams are all from Vancouver.

WOULD I LIE TO YOU? No.2

Answers

1. True.
2. True - from 1996 - 2000.
3. False - although the album packaging claimed it to be true!
4. True - Dusty was too ill to perform at the time .
5. True.
6. False - 'All around the world' by Oasis is just under ten minutes in length.
7. True.
8. False - she was born in Dunfermline, Fife.
9. True.
10. True - in 1972 with 'Long haired lover from Liverpool'.
11. False - she was with Chicken Shack.
12. True.
13. True.
14. False - he was born in London.
15. True - and they had chart success along with Bananarama.
16. True - Matchstalk men and matchstalk cats and dogs. They were 'Brian and Michael'.
17. True.
18. False - they were born in Hertford.
19. True.
20. False - Kim and Cohen are from Montreal.

JOIN TOGETHER No.2

These groups were known for backing which musician?

1. The Majors.
2. The Mince Pies.
3. The Unitone.
4. The Forbidden.
5. His Soul Band.
6. The Coconuts.
7. The Masters of ceremonies.
8. The Makers.
9. The D Cups.
10. The Romantics.
11. The Gang.
12. The Gingerbreads.
13. His Greek Serenaders.
14. The Invisible Girls.
15. The Banshees.
16. The Good Feeling.
17. Strange Behaviour.
18. The Funky Bunch.
19. The Imperials.
20. The Mindbenders.

JOIN TOGETHER No.2

Answers

1. Morris Minor.
2. Gay Gordon.
3. Laurel Aitken.
4. Jet Bronx.
5. Eddy.
6. Kid Creole.
7. DJ Pied Piper.
8. Reverend (John McClure).
9. Ivor Biggun (aka Doc Cox).
10. Ruby.
11. Kool (aka Muhammad Bayyan).
12. Goldie.
13. Makadopoulos.
14. Pauline Murray.
15. Siouxsie (Sioux).
16. Eric.
17. Jane Kennaway.
18. Markie Mark.
19. Little Anthony.
20. Wayne Fontana.

BLANK SPACE No.4

Fill in the blanks to reveal bands that have had chart hits:

1. T _ X _ S
2. N _ S _ V _ L _ E   _ E _ N _
3. S _ A _   6 _
4. N _ W   _ R _ E _
5. M _ N _ R _ N _ X
6. C _ A _   A _ D   _ A _ E
7. M _ N _ C   _ T _ E _ T   _ R _ A _ H _ R _
8. M _ G _ I _ N _ S _   F _ I _ T
9. T _ A _ S   _ O _   F _ A _ S
10. D _ A _ O _   B _ U _
11. A _ R _ S _ I _ H
12. M _ O _ Y   _ L _ E _
13. R _ G _ T   _ A _ D   _ R _ D
14. M _ T _   B _ A _ C _
15. K _ N _   B _ O _ H _ R _
16. M _ N _ O   _ E _ R _
17. S _ A _ D _ U   _ A _ L _ T
18. R _ A _ H _ O _ D
19. A _ T _ R _ D   _ M _ G _ S
20. P _ S _ Y _ A _ T   _ O _ L _

BLANK SPACE No.4

ANSWERS

1. Texas.
2. Nashville Teens.
3. Sham 69.
4. New Order.
5. Mantronix.
6. Chas and Dave.
7. Manic Street Preachers.
8. McGuinness Flint.
9. Tears for Fears.
10. Deacon Blue.
11. Aerosmith.
12. Moody Blues.
13. Right Said Fred.
14. Matt Bianco.
15. King Brothers.
16. Mungo Jerry.
17. Spandau Ballet.
18. Roachford.
19. Altered Images.
20. Pussycat Dolls.

TWO OF US No.2

Can you complete the names of these duos?

1. Addams and ?

2. Monk B and ?

3. Danny Campbell and ?

4. Lesley Garrett and ?

5. Agnelli and ?

6. Booth and ?

7. Judy Clay and ?

8. Oxide and ?

9. K-Cl and ?

10. DJ Luck and?

11. H and ?

12. Wilfred Bramble and ?

13. Svenson and ?

14. Art and Dotty ?

15. Louchie Lou and ?

16. Patrick MacNee and ?

17. Alfi and ?

18. Conductor and ?

19. Scott and ?

20. Richard Denton and ?

TWO OF US No.2

Answers

1. Gee.
2. Blade.
3. Sasha.
4. Amanda Thompson.
5. Nelson.
6. The Bad Angel.
7. William Bell.
8. Nutrino.
9. JoJo.
10. MC Neat.
11. Claire.
12. Harry H Corbett.
13. Gielen.
14. Todd.
15. Michie One.
16. Honor Blackman.
17. Harry.
18. The Cowboy.
19. Leon.
20. Martin Cook.

WHO ARE YOU? No.4

Which name is missing from these song titles?

1 _ _ _ _ _ 's the name) His latest flame (Elvis Presley)

2 Sloop _ _ _ _ B (Beach Boys)

3 _ _ _ _ _ , I'm not your daddy (Kid Creole)

4 _ _ _ _ _ _   (Barry Ryan)

5 First of _ _ _   (Bee Gees)

6 _ _ _ _ _ skies (Jesus and Mary Chain)

7 _ _ _ _, I'm only dancing (David Bowie)

8 Hat's off to _ _ _ _ _   (Del Shannon)

9 I did what I did for _ _ _ _ _   (Tony Christie)

10 _ _ _ _ _ _ _ _   (The Kinks)

11 _ _ _ _ _ 's girl (Susan Maughan)

12 Come on _ _ _ _ _ _   (Dexy's Midnight Runners)

13 _ _ _ _ _ _ Layne (Pink Floyd)

14 _ _ _ _ _ _ _   (Mark Ronson featuring Amy Winehouse)

15 _ _ _ _ _ Davis eyes (Kim Carnes)

16 Baby _ _ _ _   (Rod Stewart)

17 _ _ _ _ _   (10cc)

18 Living next door to _ _ _ _ _   (Smokie)

19 Jumpin' _ _ _ _ Flash (Rolling Stones)

20 _ _ _ _ _ _ _   (Little Richard)

WHO ARE YOU? No.4

Answers

1	Marie.
2	John.
3	Annie.
4	Eloise.
5	May.
6	April.
7	John.
8	Larry.
9	Maria.
10	Victoria.
11	Bobby.
12	Eileen.
13	Arnold.
14	Valerie.
15	Bette.
16	Jane.
17	Donna.
18	Alice.
19	Jack.
20	Lucille.

THE NAME GAME No.4

By what names are the following better known:

1. Thomas August Darnell Browder.
2. James Todd Smith.
3. Alecia Beth Moore.
4. Jacqueline McKinnon.
5. Patrick Chukwuemeka Okogwu.
6. Gerard Hugh Sayer.
7. Christa Paffgen.
8. Rory Charles Graham.
9. Ebba Tove Elsa Nilsson.
10. James Roderick Moir.
11. Charlotte Emma Aitchison.
12. Leslie Sebastian Charles.
13. Marvin Lee Aday.
14. Lynn Annette Ripley.
15. Bernard William Jewry.
16. Louise Bobb.
17. Stephen Paul Manderson.
18. Eugene Nwohia.
19. Dennis Princewell Stehr.
20. Paul Francis Gadd.

THE NAME GAME No.4

Answers

1. Kid Creole.
2. LL Cool J.
3. Pink.
4. Kelly Marie.
5. Tinie Tempah.
6. Leo Sayer.
7. Nico.
8. Rag'n'Bone Man.
9. Tove Lo.
10. Vic Reeves.
11. Charlie XCX.
12. Billy Ocean.
13. Meat Loaf.
14. Twinkle.
15. Alvin Stardust (AKA Shane Fenton).
16. Gabrielle (and that's her middle name - that we left out!).
17. Professor Green.
18. DJ Pied Piper.
19. Mr Probz.
20. Gary Glitter.

COMMON PEOPLE No.2

What do the following have in common?

1. Karen Black, Barry McGuire, Kim Carnes, Kenny Rogers, Gene Clark.

2. The life I lead, Fidelity fiduciary bank, Stay awake, A man has dreams, Step in time.

3. Mr tambourine man, Make you feel my love, All along the watchtower, The mighty Quinn, Knockin' on Heaven's door.

4. Darius Campbell, Gareth Gates, Sam and Mark, Michelle McManus, Will Young.

5. Fragile, Tormato, Fly from here, Close to the edge, Big generator.

6. China in your hand, La isla bonita, It's a sin, Nothing's gonna stop us now, You win again.

7. Erasure, Assembly, Depeche Mode, VCMG, Yazoo.

8. Make it mine, Transamazonia, Boss drum, Move any mountain, Destination Eschaton.

9. Jackie, Tito, Randy, Marlon, Jermaine.

10. Roger Glover, Steve Morse, Jon Lord, Glenn Hughes, David Coverdale.

11. The gold experience, Dirty mind, Parade, Chaos and disorder, Graffiti bridge.

12. The Hollies, Simply Red, Oasis, The Smiths, Herman's Hermits

13. Paul Arthurs, Tony McCarroll, Gem Archer, Andy Bell, Paul McGuigan.

14. Francis Rossi, Paul Weller, Phil Collins, Tony Hadley, Paul Young.

15. Viva el amor, Get close, Learning to crawl, Loose screw, Packed!

16. Jakatta, Raven Maize, Doug Willis, Sessomatto, Joey Negro.

17. The Overlanders, Storm Queen, Fern Kinney, Clive Dunn, Matthews' Southern Comfort.

18. You wear it well, Metal guru, How can I be sure?, Clair, Son of my father.

19. Jet Harris, Rod Stewart, Cozy Powell, Nicky Hopkins, Ronnie Wood.

20. Abbey Road, Help!, Let it be, Revolver, Rubber Soul.

COMMON PEOPLE No.2

ANSWERS

1. They have all been members of The New Christy Minstrels.
2. They are all songs from Mary Poppins.
3. They were all written by Bob Dylan.
4. They all had hits after appearing as contestants on Pop Idol.
5. They are all hit albums by 'Yes'.
6. They were all No.1 hits from 1987.
7. Vince Clarke was a member of all these bands.
8. They were all hit singles by The Shamen.
9. They were the Jacksons.
10. They were all members of Deep Purple.
11. They are all albums by 'Prince'.
12. They all originated from Manchester.
13. They were all members of Oasis.
14. They were all in the original Band Aid.
15. They were all hit albums by The Pretenders.
16. They were all pseudonyms used by DJ Dave Lee.
17. They all reached No.1 with their one and only hit single.
18. They were all No.1 hits from 1972.
19. They were all members of the Jeff Beck Group.
20. They are all albums by The Beatles.

EMPTY SPACES No.5

Fill in the blanks to reveal musicians who have had chart hits:

1. W_I_N_Y _O_S_O_
2. D_L _H_N_O_
3. T_R_ A_O_
4. M_C_A_L _O_T_N
5. S_M_N_H_ M_M_A
6. C_ C_ P_N_S_O_
7. P_T_R _K_L_E_N
8. B _ R_B_R_S_N
9. R_N_O _T_R_
10. Q_E_N _A_I_A_H
11. D_N_Y _S_O_D
12. E_R_H_ K_T_
13. R_B_R_ P_L_E_
14. L_A_N _I_E_
15. L_S_ S_A_F_E_D
16. C_N_A_ T_I_T_
17. J_A_ A_M_T_A_I_G
18. A_E_A_D_A _U_K_
19. D_A_E _D_Y
20. K_L_Y _A_I_

EMPTY SPACES No.5

ANSWERS

1. Whitney Houston.
2. Del Shannon.
3. Tori Amos.
4. Michael Bolton.
5. Samantha Mumba.
6. Ce Ce Peniston.
7. Peter Skellern.
8. B A Robertson.
9. Ringo Starr.
10. Queen Latifaih.
11. Donny Osmond.
12. Eartha Kitt.
13. Robert Palmer.
14. Leann Rimes.
15. Lisa Stansfield.
16. Conway Twitty.
17. Joan Armatrading.
18. Alexandra Burke.
19. Duane Eddy.
20. Kelly Marie.

WORDS No.4

Can you identify these famous songs from their opening lyrics:

1. If you, if you could return, don't let it burn don't let it fade ...

2. On a day like today, we pass the time away ....

3. I've been cheated by you since I don't know when. So, I made up my mind it must come to an end ....

4. I get up in the evening and I ain't got nothing to say. I come home in the morning .....

5. They say we're young and we don't know, we won't find out until we're grown ....

6. Candle light and soul forever, a dream of you and me together. say you believe it ....

7. And the women tug their hair like they're trying to prove it won't fall out ...

8. I remember when rock was young, me and Suzie had so much fun .....

9. Sometimes you're better off dead. There's a gun in your hand and it's pointing at your head ....

10. I looked to the sky where an elephant's eye was looking at me from a bubblegum tree ....

11. I won't let you down. I will not give you up. Gotta have some faith in the sound ....

12. At first I was afraid, I was petrified. Kept thinking I could never live without you by my side ....

13. All the girls on the block knocking at my door! Wanna know what it is make the boys want more? .....

14. In my imagination there is no complication, I dream about you all the time ....

15. You took a mystery and made me want it. You got a pedestal and put me on it ...

16. Don't know much about history, don't know much biology ......

17. I'm busy throwing hints that he keeps missing. Don't have to think about it .....

18. You get a shiver in the dark, it's raining in the park, but meantime ....

19. There's dancing behind movie scenes, behind those movie screens - saddi rani ....

20. I thought love was only true in fairytales, meant for someone else but not for me ....

WORDS No.4

Answers

1. Linger (The Cranberries).
2. Love letters in the sand (Pat Boone).
3. Mamma mia (Abba).
4. Dancing in the dark (Bruce Springsteen).
5. I got you babe (Sonny and Cher).
6. 2 become 1 (Spice Girls).
7. Rotterdam (Beautiful South).
8. Crocodile rock (Elton John).
9. West end girls (Pet Shop Boys).
10. Hole in my shoe (Traffic).
11. Freedom! 90 (George Michael).
12. I will survive (Gloria Gaynor).
13. Black magic (Little Mix).
14. I should be so lucky (Kylie Minogue).
15. Chain reaction (Diana Ross).
16. Wonderful world (Sam Cooke).
17. Push the button (Sugababes).
18. Sultans of swing (Dire Straits).
19. Brimful of Asha (Corner Shop).
20. I'm a believer (The Monkees).

MIX IT UP No.3

Can you unravel the anagrams to identify these hit making bands?

1. SHOW HIS BEAN

2. ROMAN HOT HERB FOOD

3. ALE TINS CAPER

4. LOLA IS DRUG

5. TAR ANY FIVE

6. MILDER SPY

7. EBAY TIE BOSS

8. REEF

9. BEDS A KEY PLACE

10. SHOOT UP NORA RICE

11. A CRAP PELE

12. BANTER IN ALE STATION

13. HATS ON FEN GEESE QUOTE

14. HEAR A DIDO

15. TIRED LIAM

16. MADE ROB COLD

17. SIR VAT

18. A TRIM SHOE

19. LATIN LASS

20. BLOOD WHEN SENT KICK

MIX IT UP No.3

Answers

1. WISHBONE ASH
2. BROTHERHOOD OF MAN
3. ALAN PRICE SET
4. GIRLS ALOUD
5. VANITY FARE
6. SIMPLY RED
7. BEASTIE BOYS
8. FREE
9. BLACK EYED PEAS
10. HUES CORPORATION
11. PAPER LACE
12. BEATS INTERNATIONAL
13. QUEENS OF THE STONE AGE
14. RADIOHEAD
15. DEL AMITRI
16. COLOR ME BADD
17. TRAVIS
18. AEROSMITH
19. ALL SAINTS
20. NEW KIDS ON THE BLOCK

WOULD I LIE TO YOU? No.3

Are the following statements true or false?

1. 'Spirit in the sky' has been a UK No.1 hit for Norman Greenbaum, Doctor and the Medics, and Gareth Gates.

2. Jimi Hendrix, Kenny G and Judy Collins were all born in Seattle, Washington.

3. Glen Campbell recorded with the Beach boys and toured with them as a band member.

4. 'Zeitgeist' was the title of an album by The Smashing Pumpkins, Black Sabbath, and also The Levellers.

5. Clem Burke was the drummer with Blondie.

6. 'Parklife' was Blur's first hit album.

7. 'Abracadabra' was the original title for The Beatles' 'Revolver'.

8. The Barron Knights were originally known as 'The Knights of the Round Table'.

9. Brian Molko was known by the stage name 'Bomb the bass'.

10. Cyndi Lauper was the first singer to record 'I drove all night'.

11. Drummers Pete Lucas, Michael Wilson and John Hatchman all were 'Tich' in Dave Dee, Dozy, Beaky, Mick and Tich.

12. Stephen Stills auditioned for The Monkees, and when he was turned down, he suggested his friend, Peter Tork, who got the part.

13. Jamie Kensit brought in his sister, Patsy, as singer in his band, Eighth Wonder.

14. Stacey Solomon's middle names are Golda Goldstein.

15. 'Gimme all your lovin' and 'Viva Las Vegas' were ZZ Top's only UK Top Ten hits.

16. Wishbone Ash founder members Ted Turner and Martin Turner were not related.

17. Johnny Logan was Ireland's first Eurovision Song Contest winner.

18. Pink Floyd's 'Dark side of the moon' is the biggest selling album in the world.

19. Mike McGear (Scaffold) and Paul McCartney (Beatles) are the only two brothers to have had Christmas No.1 hits.

20. Felix Burton and Simon Ratcliffe are better known as Basement Jaxxx.

WOULD I LIE TO YOU? No.3

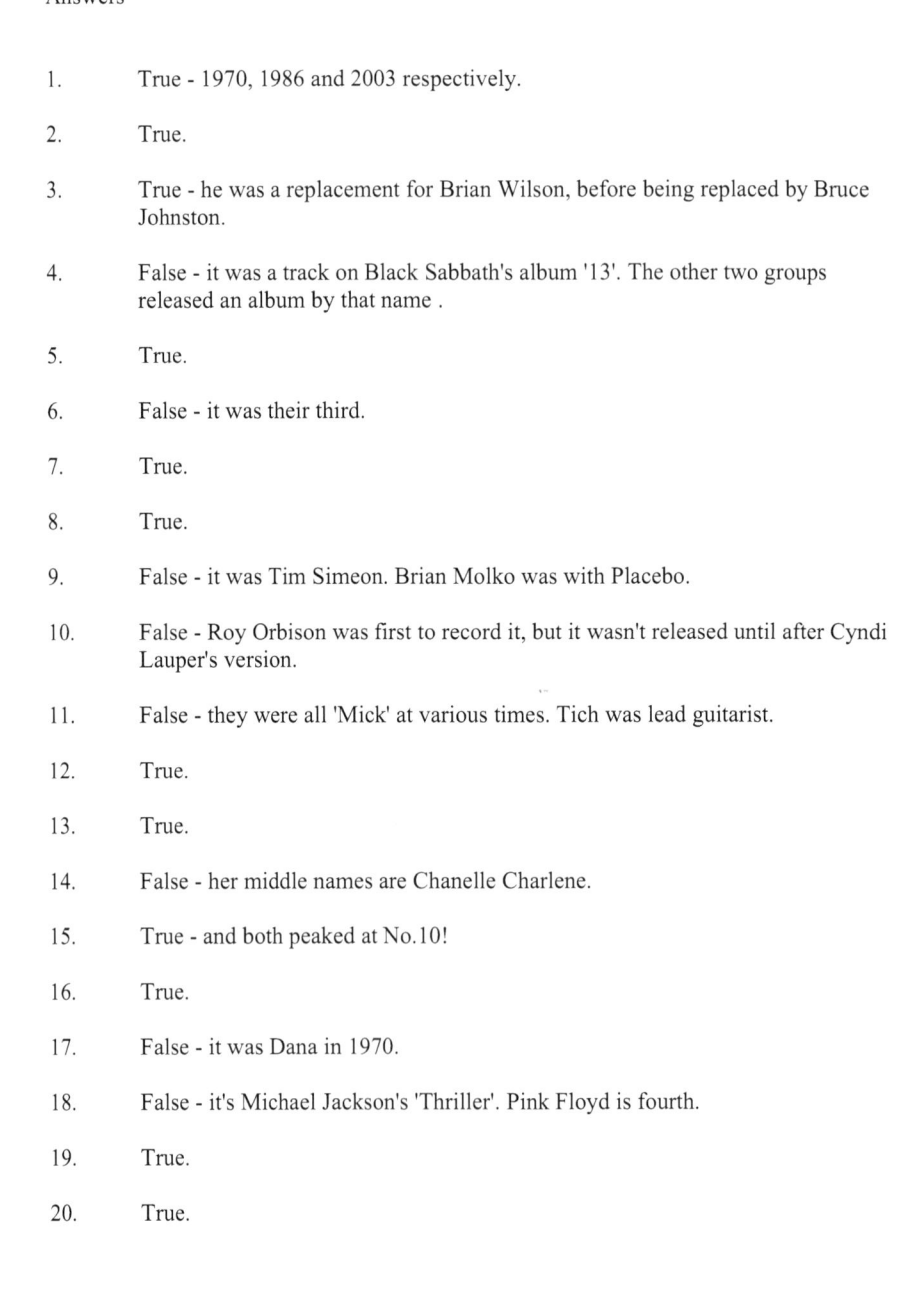

Answers

1. True - 1970, 1986 and 2003 respectively.

2. True.

3. True - he was a replacement for Brian Wilson, before being replaced by Bruce Johnston.

4. False - it was a track on Black Sabbath's album '13'. The other two groups released an album by that name .

5. True.

6. False - it was their third.

7. True.

8. True.

9. False - it was Tim Simeon. Brian Molko was with Placebo.

10. False - Roy Orbison was first to record it, but it wasn't released until after Cyndi Lauper's version.

11. False - they were all 'Mick' at various times. Tich was lead guitarist.

12. True.

13. True.

14. False - her middle names are Chanelle Charlene.

15. True - and both peaked at No.10!

16. True.

17. False - it was Dana in 1970.

18. False - it's Michael Jackson's 'Thriller'. Pink Floyd is fourth.

19. True.

20. True.

ABC No.1

The letters of the names of these groups have been arranged in alphabetical order. can you identify them?

1. CDDEEHOORSUW.
2. AADEGLMNORRSUY.
3. ABINORW.
4. ADEFIILNNRS.
5. AAEHKKLRSU.
6. AEEEGILLLOPPV.
7. ABEHNPRUY.
8. EHJLLORTTU.
9. AAGGGHILLNRSU.
10. DEFGIILNPRSS.
11. ABEGNOSVY.
12. BCCELLRTUUU.
13. DFIKLNOPY.
14. EEKMNOS.
15. AGHIIKMMNNPPSSSU.
16. ABDEGILNRTT.
17. CEGILLPRSS.
18. AACCCEEHILMMMNORY.
19. EGJMNORRUY.
20. DDGIILLOQU.

ABC No.1

Answers

1. Crowded House.
2. Royal Guardsmen.
3. Rainbow.
4. Lindisfarne.
5. Kula Shaker.
6. Village People.
7. Urban Hype.
8. Jethro Tull.
9. Sugarhill Gang.
10. Springfields
11. Vengaboys.
12. Culkture Club.
13. Pink Floyd.
14. Monkees.
15. Smashing Pumpkins.
16. Glitter Band.
17. Spice Girls.
18. My Chemical Romance.
19. Mungo Jerry.
20. Liquid Gold.

HAPPY BIRTHDAY No.3

Can you identify these musicians?

1. Singer born in Greenock, Scotland on 4 November 1963.
2. Singer / violinist born in Minsk, Belarus on 13 May 1986.
3. Singer born in Lucknow, India on 14 October 1940.
4. Singer born in Aberdeen, Scotland on 25 December 1954.
5. Guitarist born in Dartford, England on 18 December 1943.
6. Singer born in Blackpool, England on 29 September 1973.
7. Singer born in Nutbush, USA on 26 November 1939.
8. Singer born in Ibadan, Nigeria on 16 January 1959.
9. Guitarist born in Corning, USA on 26 April 1938.
10. Singer born in Skaelskor, Denmark on 11 April 1970.
11. Singer born in Knowsley, England on 25 August 1988.
12. Singer born in Honolulu, USA on 29 June 1978.
13. Singer born in Honolulu, USA on 1 December 1945.
14. Guitarist and vocalist born in Bridport, England on 9 October 1969.
15. Singer born in Paisley, Scotland on 9 January 1987.
16. Saxophonist born in Amsterdam, Netherlands on 19 September 1969.
17. Guitarist born in Barnstaple, England on 3 March 1948.
18. Singer born in Brisbane, Australia on 3 August 1970.
19. Singer born in Bangor, Wales on 29 December 1970.
20. Rapper born in Croix-des-Bouquets, Haiti on 17 October 1969.

HAPPY BIRTHDAY No.3

Answers

1. Lena Zavaroni.
2. Alexander Rybak.
3. Cliff Richard.
4. Annie Lennox.
5. Keith Richards.
6. Alfie Boe.
7. Tina Turner.
8. Sade.
9. Duane Eddy.
10. Whigfield.
11. Ray Quinn.
12. Nicole Scherzinger.
13. Bette Middler.
14. PJ Harvey.
15. Paulo Nutini.
16. Candy Dulfer.
17. Snowy White.
18. Gina G.
19. Aled Jones.
20. Wyclef Jean.

LIVIN' THING No.2

Which creatures are missing from these song titles?

1. _____ (Fleetwood Mac)
2. Chestnut ____ (The Byrds)
3. _____ love (Captain and Tennille)
4. Cool for ____ (Squeeze)
5. _____ soldier (Bob Marley)
6. ___ trap (Boomtown Rats)
7. ____ on the wing (Pink Floyd)
8. Don't kill the _____ (Yes)
9. Everybody's got something to hide except for me and my _____ (The Beatles)
10. _____ blues (The Goons)
11. Simon Smith and his amazing dancing ____ (Alan Price)
12. Cold _____ (Plastic Ono Band)
13. Honky ___ (Elton John)
14. _____ blues (Canned Heat)
15. Rockin' _____ (Michael Jackson)
16. Nellie the _____ (Toy Dolls)
17. _____ love (Donny Osmond)
18. Sugar ___ (Canned Heat)
19. (Blame it) on the ____ express (Johnny Johnson)
20. ___ out of Hell (Meat Loaf).

LIVIN' THING No.2

Answers

1. Albatross.
2. Mare.
3. Muskrat.
4. Cats.
5. Buffalo.
6. Rat.
7. Pigs.
8. Whale.
9. Monkey.
10. Bluebottle.
11. Bear.
12. Turkey.
13. Cat.
14. Bullfrog.
15. Robin.
16. Elephant.
17. Puppy.
18. Bee.
19. Pony.
20. Bat.

BLANK SPACE No.5

Fill in the blanks to reveal bands that have had chart hits:

1. O _ E _ E _ U _ L _ C
2. C _ I _ O _ Y   _ I _
3. S _ G _ A
4. 1 _ 1 _   F _ U _ T _ U _   C _ M _ A _ Y
5. A _ L   _ A _ N _ S
6. R _ X _ O _
7. J _ S _ S   _ N _   M _ R _   C _ A _ N
8. A _ O _ I _   K _ T _ E _
9. M _ T _ R _ E _ D
10. G _ L _ E _   E _ R _ I _ G
11. E _ I _ O _   L _ G _ T _ O _ S _
12. B _ 2 _
13. U _ 4 _
14. J _ F _ E _ S _ N   _ T _ R _ H _ P
15. P _ E _ A _   S _ R _ U _
16. J _ U _ N _ Y
17. D _ X _ S   _ I _ N _ G _ T   _ U _ N _ R _
18. S _ A _ E _ H _ F _ E _ S
19. J _ B _ X _ R _
20. B _ M _ A _   B _ C _ C _ E   _ L _ B

BLANK SPACE No.5

ANSWERS

1. OneRepublic.
2. Chicory Tip.
3. Sigma.
4. 1910 Fruitgum Company.
5. All Saints.
6. Rixton.
7. Jesus and Mary Chain.
8. Atomic Kitten.
9. Motorhead.
10. Golden Earring.
11. Edisdon Lighthouse.
12. B52's.
13. UB40.
14. Jefferson Starship.
15. Prefab Sprout.
16. Journey.
17. Dexy's Midnight Runners.
18. Shapeshifters.
19. Joboxers.
20. Bombay Bicycle Club.

ANY COLOUR YOU LIKE No.2

Which colour is missing from these song titles?

1	_____ room (Cream)
2	The _____ and the _____ (Amy MacDonald)
3	_____ submarine (The Beatles)
4	Sweet Georgia _____ (Ray Charles)
5	_____ velvet (Alannah Myles)
6	_____ velvet (Bobby Vinton)
7	The _____ people eater (Sheb Wooley)
8	_____ peril (Phil Lynott)
9	_____ machine (Hawkwind)
10	Band of _____ (Freda Payne)
11	_____ is _____ (Los Bravos)
12	Love is _____ (Paul Mauriat)
13	_____ sugar (Rolling Stones)
14	Lily the _____ (The Scaffold)
15	_____ or _____ (Michael Jackson)
16	_____ tie _____ noise (David Bowie)
17	_____ (Donovan)
18	Forever in _____ jeans (Neil Diamond)
19	_____ pudding Bertha (Goodies)
20	_____ (Da Ba Dee) (Eifel 65)

ANY COLOUR YOU LIKE No.2

Answers

1	White.
2	Green, blue.
3	Yellow.
4	Brown.
5	Black.
6	Blue.
7	Purple.
8	Yellow.
9	Silver.
10	Gold.
11	Black, black.
12	Blue.
13	Brown.
14	Pink.
15	Black, white.
16	Black, white.
17	Turquiose.
18	Blue.
19	Black.
20	Blue.

ALPHABET No.1

The letters of the names of these recording artists have been arranged in alphabetical order. can you identify them?

1. ABCEEGLLLMNP.

2. AAEEEHNNOSST.

3. BEEIIILLPPR.

4. EEEGINNPTY.

5. BEHNOORTT.

6. AAAEEFGHKLRRSY.

7. AEJJNOSX.

8. ABDDEIIOVW.

9. ADEFKLNRSTUUX.

10. ADEHJNOORSW.

11. ACCCEEHIMMNNORTTU.

12. AEEILMNNRS.

13. ABEHMRSSTUY.

14. AACEILNPR.

15. CEIJMOSSY.

16. AAEEEJLLSTV.

17. AADILNRSSTTUV.

18. AACDEIILLPSW.

19. AEELLLPRUW.

20. AAIKMNNOORSUU.

ALPHABET No.1

Answers

1. Glen Campbell.
2. Sheena Easton.
3. Billy Piper.
4. Gene Pitney.
5. Beth Orton.
6. Feargal Sharkey.
7. Jax Jones.
8. David Bowie.
9. Funkstar De Lux.
10. Howard Jones.
11. Martine McCutcheon.
12. Leann Rimes.
13. Busta Rhymes.
14. Alan Price.
15. Joyce Sims.
16. Taja Sevelle.
17. Alvin Stardust.
18. Lewis Capaldi.
19. Paul Weller.
20. Nana Mouskouri.

WHO ARE YOU? No.5

Which name is missing from these song titles?

1 _____ Dagger (The Fratellis)

2 _____ (Four Pennies)

3 From a ____ to a king (Ned Miller)

4 _____ ____ (Bruce Springsteen)

5 Ode to _____ ___ (Bobbie Gentry)

6 _____ ____ (Michael Jackson)

7 ___ Dooley (Lonnie Donegan)

8 The ____ and I (10cc)

9 _____ (Kenny Rogers)

10 Good grief _____ (Chicory Tip)

11 _____ (Rolling Stones)

12 ____ the pink (The Scaffold)

13 Second hand ____ (Barbra Streisand)

14 _____ (Tyanasaurus Rex)

15 _____ from the block (Jennifer Lopez)

16 Who's _____ ? (Busted)

17 _____ plain (Roxy Music)

18 ____ & _____ (John Cougar)

19 _____ and son (Cat Stevens)

20 Black _____ (Ram Jam)

WHO ARE YOU? No.5

Answers

1	Chelsea.
2	Juliet.
3	Jack.
4	Bobby Jean.
5	Billie Joe.
6	Billie Jean.
7	Tom.
8	Dean.
9	Lucille.
10	Christina.
11	Angie ... or ... Carol.
12	Lily.
13	Rose.
14	Debora.
15	Jenny.
16	David.
17	Virginia.
18	Jack, Diane.
19	Matthew.
20	Betty.

THE NAME GAME No.5

By what names are the following better known:

1. Michael Stafford.
2. Manfred Sepse Lubowitz.
3. Craig Dimech.
4. Grace Barnett Wing.
5. Emanuela Trane.
6. Robin Peter Smith.
7. Marianne Joan Elliott-Said.
8. Michael Ebenazer Kwadjo Omari Owuo.
9. James Marcus Smith.
10. Pauline Matthews.
11. John Lewis.
12. Yvette Marie Stevens.
13. Quentin Leo Cook.
14. Lili-Marlene Premilovich.
15. Victoria Loren Kelly.
16. Robert Earl Bell.
17. Richard Marshall.
18. Roger Francios Jouret.
19. Jessica Ellen Cornish.
20. Harry Wayne Casey.

THE NAME GAME No.5

Answers

1. Maverick Sabre.
2. Manfred Mann.
3. Meck.
4. Grace Slik.
5. Dolcenera.
6. Crispian St Peters.
7. Poly Styrene.
8. Stormzy.
9. P J Proby.
10. Kiki Dee.
11. Jona Lewie.
12. Chaka Khan.
13. Fat Boy Slim.
14. Lene Lovich.
15. Tori Kelly.
16. Kool (aka Muhammad Bayyan).
17. Scanty Sandwich.
18. Plastic Bertrand.
19. Jessie J.
20. KC.

ALL SHOOK UP No.3

Can you unravel the anagrams to identify these music personalities?

1. FAN RAN LIKE HART
2. BRINGS OUT ALL EVIL
3. REAL IN CAP
4. DATA SO LAME
5. BE MUCH LIABLE
6. MEDAL OR RACE
7. TRY BONE SPILL
8. SICK AI RASH
9. ONLY FAT RULED
10. AIMS ON NINE
11. BARMY IAN
12. CATCH ANY PRAM
13. SEEN CAR JOG
14. SINGED BOBBIE
15. ARAN AID RANGE
16. ASK RIK WHEN
17. AIM BRAVE HIT COCK
18. ONCE I EAT ALL
19. LIKED CORE
20. JAIL BY GERM

ALL SHOOK UP No.3

Answers

1. ARETHA FRANKLIN
2. GILBERT O'SULLIVAN
3. ALAN PRICE
4. OLETA ADAMS
5. MICHAEL BUBLE
6. CARO EMERALD
7. BILLY PRESTON
8. CHRIS ISAAK
9. NELLY FURTADO
10. NINA SIMONE
11. BRIAN MAY
12. TRACY CHAPMAN
13. GRACE JONES
14. DEBBIE GIBSON
15. ARIANA GRANDE
16. NIK KERSHAW
17. VICTORIA BECKHAM
18. NATALIE COLE
19. KID CREOLE
20. MARY J BLIGE

EMPTY SPACES No.6

Fill in the blanks to reveal musicians who have had chart hits:

1. M _ R _ E _ S _ O _ D
2. F _ A _ K _ E _ A _ L _
3. H _ L _ N _ H _ P _ R _
4. A _ D _ E _ G _ L _
5. B _ R _ S _ A _ D _ N _ R
6. A _ N _ E _ E _ N _ X
7. P _ T _ R _ E _ L _ R _
8. P _ T _ L _ C _ A _ K
9. A _ I _ I _ K _ Y _
10. D _ S _ C _ N _ O _
11. M _ R _ A _ M _ N _
12. B _ L _ I _ P _ P _ R
13. L _ U _ S _ R _ S _ R _ N _
14. C _ R _ S _ O _ T _ Z
15. B _ L _ N _ A _ A _ L _ S _ E
16. G _ R _ O _ G _ L _ R _ P
17. C _ A _ L _ S _ Z _ A _ O _ R
18. T _ R _ N _ E _ R _ N _ D _ R _ Y
19. O _ E _ A _ D _ M _
20. L _ C _ A _ O _ A _ A _ O _ T _

EMPTY SPACES No.6

ANSWERS

1. Marie Osmond.
2. Frankie Valli.
3. Helen Shapiro.
4. Andrew Gold.
5. Boris Gardiner.
6. Annie Lennox.
7. Peter Sellers.
8. Petula Clark.
9. Alicia Keys.
10. Des O'Connor.
11. Marc Almond.
12. Billie Piper.
13. Louis Armstrong.
14. Chris Montez.
15. Belinda Carlisle.
16. Gordon Giltrap.
17. Charle3s Aznavour.
18. Terrence Trent D'Arby.
19. Oleta Adams.
20. Luciano Pavarotti.

JOIN TOGETHER No.3

These groups were known for backing which musician?

1. The First Edition.
2. The Big Sound.
3. The Dreamers.
4. The Supremes.
5. The Medics.
6. The Racketeers.
7. His Jazzmen.
8. The Jordanaires.
9. The Family Stone.
10. The Ram Jam Band.
11. The Blue Flames.
12. The Attractions.
13. The E Street Band.
14. The Vandellas.
15. The Tremeloes.
16. The Luvvers.
17. The Vagabonds.
18. The Blockheads.
19. The Silver Bullet Band.
20. The Rebel Rousers.

JOIN TOGETHER No.3

Answers

1. Kenny Rogers.
2. Simon Dupree.
3. Freddie (Garrity).
4. Diana Ross.
5. (The) Doctor.
6. Elbow Bones.
7. Kenny Ball.
8. Elvis Presley.
9. Sly (Stone).
10. Geno Washington.
11. Georgie Fame (they also backed Billy Fury) ... or Jimmy James (aka Jimi Hendrix).
12. Elvis Costello.
13. Bruce Springsteen.
14. Martha Reeves.
15. Brian Poole.
16. Lulu.
17. Jimmy James (not the Jimi Hendrix one!).
18. Ian Dury.
19. Bob Seger.
20. Cliff Bennett.

WORDS No.5

Can you identify these famous songs from their opening lyrics:

1. Over Bridge of Sighs, to rest my eyes in shades of green. Under dreaming spires ...

2. No one could make me feel like this. I'm thrown and overblown with bliss ....

3. Driving down an endless road, taking friends or moving alone ....

4. When I die and they lay me to rest, gonna go to the place that's best .....

5. Everybody says it'll be okay. But I don't know when that day will come ....

6. You shake my nerves and you rattle my brain. Too much love drives a man insane ...

7. Good morning miss. Can I help you son? Sixteen today, and up for fun ...

8. I remember when, I remember, I remember when I lost my mind .....

9. Didn't know what time it was the lights were low, I leaned back on my radio ....

10. Every night in my dreams, I see you, I feel you. That is how I know you go on ....

11. I need love, love to ease my mind. I need to find, find someone to call mine ....

12. Tied. Tongue tied or short of breath, don't even try. Try a little harder ....

13. If you see me walking down the street, staring at the sky and dragging my two feet, you just pass me by .....

14. Come and look out through the window, that big old moon is shining down ....

15. All this talk of getting old. It's getting me down my love, like a cat in a bag ...

16. Sunshine came softly a-through my a-window today. Could have tripped out easy ......

17. "I wanna talk to you" "The last time we talked, Mr Smith, you reduced me to tears. I promise you it won't happen again" Do I attract you? Do I repulse you .....

18. Your eyes tell me how you love me. Can feel it in your heartbeat ....

19. Look into my eyes - you will see what you mean to me. Search your heart ....

20. We don't need no education. We don't need no thought control. No dark sarcasm in the classroom ....

WORDS No.5

Answers

1. Itchycoo Park (Small Faces).
2. There must be an angel (playing with my heart) (Eurythmics).
3. Fairground (Simply Red).
4. Spirit in the sky (Norman Greenbaum).
5. Happy (Pharrell Williams).
6. Great balls of fire (Jerry Lee Lewis).
7. House of fun (Madness).
8. Crazy (Gnarls Barkley).
9. Starman (David Bowie).
10. My heart will go on (Celine Dion).
11. You can't hurry love (The Supremes).
12. Too shy (Kajagoogoo).
13. Whole again (Atomic Kitten).
14. Blanket on the ground (Billie Jo Spears).
15. The drugs don't work (The Verve).
16. Sunshine Superman (Donovan).
17. Grace Kelly (Mika).
18. Jump (for my love) (Pointer Sisters).
19. (Everything I do) I do it for you (Bryan Adams).
20. Another brick in the wall (Part II) (Pink Floyd).

THERE'S A PLACE No.3

Which place name is missing from these song titles?

1   _ _ _ _ _ _ _   Avenue (Duffy)

2   _ _ _ _ _ _ _ _ _ _   Road (David Tomlinson)

3   From _ _ _ _ _ _ _ to _ _ (Patsy Gallant)

4   _ _ _ _ _   girl (David Bowie)

5   I don't want to go to _ _ _ _ _ _ _ (Elvis Costello)

6   _ _ _ _ _ _ _ _ _ _ _ (Christie)

7   Last train to _ _ _ _ _ _ _ _ _ _ (The Monkees)

8   Last train to _ _ _ _ _ _ _ _ _ _ (Johnny Duncan)

9   Last train to _ _ _ _ _ _ _ Central (Billy Connolly)

10   _ _ _ _ _ _ _ _ _ _ Fair / Canticle (Simon and Garfunkel)

11   (The leaving) _ _ _ _ _ _ town (Roger Whittaker)

12   _ _ _ _ (Gibson Brothers)

13   _ _ _ _ _ _   tea party (Sensational Alex Harvey Band)

14   Streets of _ _ _ _ _ _ _ _ _ _ _ _ (Bruce Springsteen)

15   Streets of _ _ _ _ _ _ (Ralph McTell)

16   _ _ _ _ _ _ _ _   plain (Roxy Music)

17   _ _ _ _ _ _ _ _ _ _ _ _ _ (Wings)

18   Blue _ _ _ _ _ _ (Elvis Presley)

19   Living in America (James Brown)

20   _ _ _ _ _ _ _ _ rock (Queen)

THERE'S A PLACE No.3

Answers

1	Warwick.
2	Portobello.
3	New York, LA.
4	China.
5	Chelsea.
6	San Bernadino.
7	Clarksville.
8	San Fernando.
9	Glasgow.
10	Scarborough.
11	Durham.
12	Cuba.
13	Boston.
14	Philadelphia.
15	London.
16	Virginia..
17	Mull of Kintyre.
18	Hawaii.
19	America.
20	Brighton.

BLANK SPACE No.6

Fill in the blanks to reveal bands that have had chart hits:

1. T _ R _ E   _ E _ R _ E _
2. H _ W _ W _ N _
3. P _ R _ N _ R _   I _   K _ Y _ E
4. C _ I _ K _ N   _ H _ C _
5. C _ R _ O _ I _ Y   _ I _ L _ D   _ H _   C _ T
6. S _ O _ A _ D _ W _ D _ Y
7. N _ W   _ I _ S   _ N   _ H _   B _ O _ K
8. G _ O _ O _ M
9. J _   J _   G _ N _ E
10. P _ A _ E _ O
11. M _ D _ C _ N _   H _ A _
12. S _ R _ T _ I   _ O _ I _ T _
13. F _ N _ Y   _ O _ M
14. P _ P   _ I _ L   _ A _   I _ S _ L _
15. H _ Y _ I   _ A _ T _ Y _ E _
16. M _ D _ R _   R _ M _ N _ E
17. C _ O _ T
18. T _ I _ T _ D   _ I _ T _ R
19. O _ T _ W _ N
20. G _ R _ Y _   Z _ G _ T _ C   _ Y _ C _

BLANK SPACE No.6

ANSWERS

1. Three Degrees
2. Hawkwind.
3. Partnerz in Kryme
4. Chicken Shack.
5. Curiosity Killed The Cat.
6. Showaddywaddy.
7. New Kids on the Block.
8. Gloworm.
9. Jo Jo Gunne.
10. Placebo.
11. Medicine Head.
12. Scritti Politti.
13. Funky Worm.
14. Pop Will Eat Itself.
15. Haysi Fantayzee.
16. Modern Romance.
17. Clout.
18. Twisted Sister.
19. Ottowan.
20. Gorkys Zygotic Mynci.

LUCKY NUMBER No.3

Which cardinal or ordinal numbers are missing from these song titles?

1. _____ tribes (Frankie goes to Hollywood)
2. The _____ teens (Sweet)
3. _____ miles (The Pretenders)
4. _____ - _____ - _____ - _____ - _____ (Manfred Mann)
5. Pigs (_____ different ones) (Pink Floyd)
6. Fields of fire (_____ miles) (Big Country)
7. _____ years in Tibet (David Bowie)
8. _____ of us (The Beatles)
9. _____ in _____ (808 State)
10. _____ overture (Electric Light Orchestra)
11. _____ tons (Tennessee Ernie Ford)
12. Mary of the _____ form (Boomtown Rats)
13. _____ (Mansun)
14. The _____ of never (Donny Osmond)
15. _____ - _____ - _____ - _____ motorway (Tom Robinson Band)
16. A _____ love songs (Take That)
17. _____ miles an hour (New Order)
18. _____ or _____ to _____ (Chicago)
19. _____ seasons of loneliness (Boyz II Men)
20. Conversations with my _____ year old self (Pink)

LUCKY NUMBER No.3

Answers

1	Two.
2	Six.
3	Two thousand.
4	Five, four, three, two, one.
5	Three.
6	Four hundred.
7	Seven.
8	Two.
9	One, ten.
10	One, Zero, Five, Three, Eight.
11	Sixteen.
12	Fourth.
13	Six.
14	Twelfth.
15	Two, Four, Six, Eight.
16	Million.
17	Sixty.
18	Twenty five, Six, Four.
19	Four.
20	Thirteen.

YOU'RE THE ONE No.2

Can you spot the odd one out in each case?

1. One trick pony, Step two, Crepes and drapes, Red star, Bright lights .

2. Pointer Sisters, Everly Brothers, White Stripes, Yazoo, Go West.

3. Mr Blobby, Oh Carolina, Living on my own, All that she wants, Breakfast at Tiffany's.

4. Mikael Rickfors, Carl Wayne, Tobias Forge, Alan Clarke, Peter Howarth.

5. Neil Diamond, Christina Aguilera, 50 Cent, Tony Bennett, Belinda Carlisle.

6. Rick West, Alan Blakley, Dave Munden, Chip Hawkes, Pete Staples.

7. The damned don't cry, Mind of a toy, Ship of fools, Pleasure boys, Night train.

8. Come fly with me, I remember Tommy, Come dance with me, I'll remember you, Come swing with me.

9. Jason Bonham, Luke Johnson, Nigel Clark, Harry Styles, Les Gray.

10. Mr Bojangles, Red red wine, Sweet Caroline, You don't bring me flowers, I'm a believer.

11. The wonder of you, Rubber bullets, Woodstock, Back home, All kinds of everything.

12. Malcolm Allured, Buddy Gask, Romeo Challenger, Den Hegarty, Russ Field.

13. Zara Larsson, The Cardigans, Focus, Abba, Eagle-Eye Cherry.

14. On every street, On the border, Desperado, The long run, Long road out of Eden.

15. We are young, Crazy stupid love, Titanium, Bom bom, Part of me.

16. Melanie Blatt, Jon Lee, Tina Barrett, Paul Cattermole, Rachel Stevens.

17. Beat it, Human nature, Another part of me, Billie Jean, Wanna be startin' somethin'.

18. Start me up, Honky tonk women, Fool to cry, Brown sugar, Little red rooster.

19. Calum Hood, Ryan Tedder, Ashton Irwin, Michael Clifford, Luke Hemmings.

20. Shoot to thrill, You shook me all night long, Have a drink on me, Shot down in flames, Given the dog a bone.

YOU'RE THE ONE No.2

ANSWERS

1. One trick pony - is an album by Paul Simon, the others are by Showaddywaddy.

2. Pointer Sisters - have always had three or more members, the rest are duos.

3. Breakfast at Tiffany's - was No.1 in 1996, the others topped the chart in 1993.

4. Tobias Forge - the rest have all been lead singer with The Hollies.

5. Belinda Carlisle - is from Los Angeles, the others are New Yorkers.

6. Peter Staples - was with The Troggs, the others were The Tremeloes.

7. Ship of fools - was a hit single for Erasure, the others were by Visage.

8. I'll remember you - is an album by Frank Ifield, the others are Frank Sinatra albums.

9. Les Gray - is from Carshalton, the others are from Redditch.

10. Mr Bojangles - was written by Jerry Jeff Walker, the others were written (or co-written) by Neil Diamond.

11. Rubber bullets - was No.1 in 1973, the others topped the chart in 1970.

12. Den Hegarty - was with Darts, the others were with Showaddywaddy.

13. Focus - is a Dutch group, the others are Swedish.

14. On every street - was an album by Dire Straits, the others are by The Eagles.

15. Crazy stupid love - was No.1 in 2014, the others topped the chart in 2012.

16. Melanie Blatt - was in All Saints, the others were S Club 7.

17. Another part of me - is from Michael Jackson's album 'Bad', the others are from 'Thriller'.

18. Little red rooster - was written by Willie Dixon, the others were by Mick Jagger and Keith Richard.

19. Ryan Tedder- was with One republic - the others with 5 Seconds of Summer.

20. Shot down in Flames - was from AC/DC's 'Highway to hell', the others were from 'Back in black'.

WHO ARE YOU? No.6

Which name is missing from these song titles?

1   _ _ _ _ Tuesday (Rolling Stones)

2   Dear _ _ _ _ _ _ _ _ (Foo Fighters)

3   _ _ _ _ _ _ _ (Status Quo)

4   _ _ _ _ _ the spider (The Who)

5   Careful with that axe, _ _ _ _ _ _ (Pink Floyd)

6   _ _ _ _ _ _ (Foster and Allen)

7   _ _ _ _ _ (Blue Mink)

8   The ballad of _ _ _ _ _ _ and _ _ _ _ _ (Georgie Fame)

9   A boy named _ _ _ (Johnny Cash)

10 _ _ _ _ 's tartan army (Andy Cameron)

11 _ _ _ _ _ _ _ (The Police)

12 I'm _ _ _ _ _ the VIII, I am (Herman's Hermits)

13 Doctor _ _ _ _ _ _ (The Beatles)

14 _ _ _ _ _ _ (Simon and Garfunkel)

15 The days of Pearly _ _ _ _ _ _ _ (Marc Almond)

16 _ _ _ _ _   _ _ _ (Buddy Holly)

17 Viva _ _ _ _ _   _ _ _ (The Equals)

18 _ _ _ _ 's boy child (Boney M)

19 _ _ _ _ _ _ _ _ _ (Four Tops)

20 Telegram _ _ _ (T Rex)

WHO ARE YOU? No.6

Answers

1   Ruby.
2   Rosemary.
3   Caroline.
4   Boris.
5   Eugene.
6   Maggie.
7   Randy.
8   Bonnie, Clyde.
9   Sue.
10 Ally.
11 Roxanne.
12 Henry.
13 Robert.
14 Cecilia.
15 Spencer.
16 Peggy Sue.
17 Bobby Joe.
18 Mary.
19 Bernadette.
20 Sam.

HAPPY BIRTHDAY No.4

Can you identify these musicians?

1. Singer born in Londonderry, Northern Ireland on 13 August 1958.
2. Keyboard player born in London, England on 3 July 1960.
3. Singer born in Madrid, Spain on 8 May 1975.
4. Drummer born in Chelmsford, England on 23 December 1985.
5. Singer born in Dublin, Ireland on 3 March 1977.
6. Singer born in Whitburn, Scotland on 30 December 1988.
7. Singer born in Kutaisi, Georgia on 16 September 1984.
8. Guitarist born in Brenchley, England on 6 April 1948.
9. Singer born in Haywards Heath, England on 26 November 1981.
10. Singer born in Burnaby, Canada on 9 September 1975.
11. DJ born in Dartford, England on 30 July 1960.
12. Singer born in Ballybricken, Ireland on 6 September 1971.
13. Singer born in Nottingham, England on 28 February 1994.
14. Singer born in Stockholm, Sweden on 10 March 1964.
15. Drummer born in Colchester, England on 8 May 1964.
16. Singer born in Amsterdam, Netherlands on 26 April 1981.
17. Guitarist born in Glasgow, Scotland on 31 March 1955.
18. Singer born in Southampton, England on 5 May 1981.
19. Singer born in New York, USA on 24 April 1942.
20. Rapper born in Kingston, Jamaica on 9 January 1973.

HAPPY BIRTHDAY No.4

Answers

1. Feargal Sharkey.
2. Vince Clarke.
3. Enrique Iglesias.
4. Harry Judd.
5. Ronan Keating.
6. Leon Jackson.
7. Katie Melua.
8. Gordon Giltrap.
9. Natasha Beddingfield.
10. Michael Buble.
11. Pete Tong.
12. Dolores O'Riordan.
13. Jake Bugg.
14. Neneh Cherry.
15. Dave Rowntree.
16. Caro Emerald.
17. Angus Young.
18. Craig David.
19. Barbra Streisand.
20. Sean Paul.

EMPTY SPACES No.7

Fill in the blanks to reveal musicians who have had chart hits:

1. A _ I _ N _   G _ A _ D _
2. G _ Y   _ I _ C _ E _ L
3. C _ R I _   M _ Y _ I _ L _
4. T _ A _ Y   _ H _ P _ A _
5. R _ C _ A _ D   _ R _ X
6. J _ C _ L _ N   _ R _ W _
7. G _ A _ E   _ O _ E _
8. D _ B _ I _   G _ B _ O _
9. R _ L _ H   _ R _ D _ E
10. M _ X _ N _   N _ G _ T _ N _ A _ E
11. J _ L _ A   _ O _ D _ A _
12. E _ D _ E   _ O _ M _
13. N _ N _ H   _ H _ R _ Y
14. G _ O _ G _ O   _ O _ O _ E _
15. R _ B _ R _ A   _ L _ C _
16. R _ N _ I _   C _ R _ O _ L
17. R _ C _   A _ T _ E _
18. H _ R _ Y   _ E _ A _ O _ T _
19. V _ C _ O _ I _   B _ C _ H _ M
20. A _ K _ R   _ I _ K

EMPTY SPACES No.7

ANSWERS

1. Ariana Grande.
2. Guy Mitchell.
3. Curtis Mayfield.
4. Tracy Chapman.
5. Richard Marx.
6. Jocelyn Brown.
7. Grace Jones.
8. Debbie Gibson.
9. Ralph Fridge.
10. Maxine Nightingale.
11. Julia Fordham.
12. Eydie Gorme.
13. Neneh Cherry.
14. Giorgio Moroder.
15. Roberta Flack.
16. Ronnie Carroll.
17. Rick Astley.
18. Harry Belafonte.
19. Victoria Beckham.
20. Acker Bilk.

THE NAME GAME No.6

By what names are the following better known:

1. Derek William Dick.
2. Mary Aiese O'Leary.
3. Francesco Paolo LoVecchio.
4. Clive Jackson.
5. Chester Arthur Burnett.
6. Glyn Geoffrey Ellis.
7. Morgan Geist.
8. Charles Weedon Westover.
9. Calvin Cordozar Broadus.
10. Dana Elaine Owens.
11. Sylvester Stewart.
12. Trevor George Smith.
13. Harry Rodger Webb.
14. David Andrew Burd.
15. Declan Patrick MacManus.
16. Omar Samuel Pasley.
17. Elaine Bookbinder.
18. Ayodeji Ibrahim Balogun.
19. Sally Olwen Clark.
20. Graham McPherson.

THE NAME GAME No.6

Answers

1. Fish.
2. Reparata.
3. Frankie Laine.
4. The Doctor.
5. Howlin' Wolf.
6. Wayne Fontana.
7. Storm Queen.
8. Del Shannon.
9. Snoop Dog.
10. Queen Latifiah.
11 Sly Stone.
12. Busta Rhymes.
13. Cliff Richard.
14. Lil Dickie.
15. Elvis Costello.
16. OMI.
17. Elkie Brooks.
18. Wizkid.
19. Petula Clark.
20. Suggs.

MIX IT UP No.4

Can you unravel the anagrams to identify these hit making bands?

1. AYE RASH
2. PINK SLOT
3. FOUR IN ROAD RACING AT TT
4. TRUE BMW YA YA
5. CHESTY LIDS DIN
6. GAMMON NOR LARD
7. FACE A RIDER
8. INTO TICK TEAM
9. ABLE COP
10. CORNER DOME MAN
11. GIN JUGS IN NEW BALES
12. FED RICK A VALVE
13. STERN FIFE JAR SHOPS
14. YES FIFA WON NO TUNA
15. BEG SLUG
16. ARAB EGG
17. ERE TRY LESS VIBES
18. PACK LEG BAR
19. SOON FEAR IT
20. CRYING BOUT

MIX IT UP No.4

Answers

1. HEAR SAY
2. SLIPKNOT
3. FAIRGROUND ATTRACTION
4. TUBEWAY ARMY
5. DESTINY'S CHILD
6. LONDON GRAMMAR
7. ARCADE FIRE
8. ATOMIC KITTEN
9. PLACEBO
10. MODERN ROMANCE
11. SWINGING BLUE JEANS
12. DAVE CLARK FIVE
13. JEFFERSON STARSHIP
14. FOUNTAINS OF WAYNE
15. BUGGLES
16. GARBAGE
17. BEVERLEY SISTERS
18. BLACK GRAPE
19. ART OF NOISE
20. BIG COUNTRY

THE FIRST No.2

1. What was the first Top Ten single by Franz Ferdinand?
2. Whose first album was called 'Lights'?
3. 'Looking after No.1' was the first Top Ten single for which group?
4. Who was the original drummer with Oasis?
5. What was the title of the first hit record for the Kinks?
6. Who was the founder and original guitarist and leader of the Rolling Stones?
7. What was Bob Marley's first Top Ten hit?
8. What was the first track on Pulp's 'Different class'?
9. Whose first hit was 'Look what they done to my song, Ma'?
10. Who was the first British singer to have three successive UK chart No.1 singles?
11. What was the wanted first hit single?
12. Whose first hit single was 'Don't dream it's over'?
13. Stone Gon' was the title of whose first hit album?
14. What was the title of Chris Rea's first hit single?
15. Clem Curtis was the original singer with which chart topping group?
16. What was the title of Don McLean's first UK No.1?
17. What was the title of Human League's first No.1 album?
18. Whose first No.1 was 'My chico latino'?
19. What is the opening track on Madonna's 'Like a virgin' album'?
20. Whose first album was called 'Generation Terrorists'?

THE FIRST No.2

Answers

1. Take me out.
2. Ellie Goulding.
3. Boomtown Rats.
4. Tony McCarroll.
5. Long Tall Sally.
6. Brian Jones.
7. No woman, no cry (after 13 years and an incredible 98 singles!).
8. Mis-shapes.
9. New Seekers.
10. Frank Ifield.
11. All time low.
12. Crowded House.
13. Barry White.
14. Fool (if you think it's over).
15. The Foundations.
16. Vincent.
17. Dare.
18. Geri Halliwell.
19. Material Girl.
20. Manic Street Preachers.

WORDS No.6

Can you identify these famous songs from their opening lyrics:

1. Wake up in the morning with a head like 'What ya done?' ...
2. Watch it! I was born in a crossfire hurricane, and I howled at my ma ....
3. Some people call me the space cowboy, yeah, some call me the gangster of love ....
4. I believe the children are our future. Teach them well and let them lead the way ....
5. Come up to meet you, tell you I'm sorry. You don't know how lovely you are ....
6. Here comes Johnny Yen again with the liquor and drugs and a flesh machine . ...
7. Juat a castaway, an island lost at sea. Another lonely day with no one here but me .....
8. There's a boy, a little boy shooting arrows in the blue, and he's aiming them .....
9. A great philosopher once wrote naughty, naughty, very naughty ....
10. Well, you're dirty and sweet, clad in black, don't look back, and I love you ...
11. Well, we know where we're going, but we don't know where we've been ....
12. Let's go girls, come on! I'm going out tonight - I'm feelin' alright ....
13. I'm a-gonna raise a fuss, I'm a-gonna raise a holler, about workin' all summer .....
14. We'll do it all. Everything on our own. We don't need anything or anyone ....
15. Does she walk? Does she talk? Does she come complete? My homeroom, homeroom angel ...
16. Oh, my life is changing every day, in every possible way ....
17. Oh, is he more, too much more, than a pretty face? It's so strange the way he talking, it's a disgrace .....
18. You say you wander your own land. But when I think about it, I don't se how you can ....
19. Two. One, two, three, four. Ev'rybody's talking about bagism, shagism, dragism ....
20. Sometimes the river flows but nothing breathes. A train arrives but never leaves ....

WORDS No.6

Answers

1. I don't feel like dancing (Scissor Sisters).

2. Jumpin' Jack Flash (Rolling Stones).

3. The joker (Steve Miller Band).

4. Greatest love of all (Whitney Houston).

5. The Scientst (Coldplay).

6. Lust for life (Iggy Pop).

7. Message in a bottle (The Police).

8. Little arrows (Leapy Lee).

9. Ebeneezer Goode (The Shamen).

10. Get it on (T Rex).

11. Road to nowhere (Talking Heads).

12. Man! I feel like a woman! (Shania Twain).

13. Summertime blues (Eddie Cochran).

14. Chasing cars (Snow Patrol).

15. Centrefold (J Geils Band).

16. Dreams (The Cranberries).

17. I'm gonna make you a star (David Essex).

18. Everybody's changing (Keane).

19. Give peace a chance (Plastic Ono Band).

20. Search for the hero (M People).

WE ARE FAMILY No.2

Which human relations are missing from these song titles?

1. Tie your _____ down (Queen)
2. ___ of my _____ (Chicory Tip)
3. Take your _____ .... to the slaughter (Iron Maiden)
4. __ Baker (Boney M)
5. _____ Louie (Hot Chocolate)
6. Evil ____ (Eminem)
7. _____ are doin' it for themselves (Eurythmics and Aretha Franklin)
8. _____ and ___ (Cat Stevens)
9. Your _____ Grizelda (The Monkees)
10. Kissin' _____ (Elvis Presley)
11. I saw a man and he danced with his ____ (Cher)
12. _____ Albert (Paul and Linda McCartney)
13. _____ of mine (Neil Reid)
14. Dear future _____ (Meghan Trainor)
15. Listen to your _____ (Feargal Sharkey)
16. Sail away sweet _____ (Queen)
17. _____ and child reunion (Paul Simon)
18. _____ 's party (Paul Nicholas)
19. _____ 's party (Monie Love)
20. Big _____ (Kanye West).

WE ARE FAMILY No.2

Answers

1   Mother.
2   Son, father.
3   Daughter.
4   Ma.
5   Brother.
6   Twin.
7   Sisters.
8   Father, son.
9   Auntie.
10 Cousins.
11 Wife.
12 Uncle.
13 Mother.
14 Husband.
15 Father.
16 Sister.
17 Mother.
18 Grandma.
19 Grandpa.
20 Brother.

TWO OF US No.3

Can you complete the names of these duos?

1. Peters and ?
2. Yarbrough and ?
3. Paul and ?
4. John Travolta and ?
5. Ant and ?
6. PJ and ?
7. Jack and ?
8. Hale and ?
9. Renee and ?
10. Rene and?
11. Rob Bass and ?
12. Mel and ?
13. Scott Fitzgerald and ?
14. Dick and ?
15. Brian and ?
16. Womack and ?
17. Bob and ?
18. Bell and ?
19. Heavy D and ?
20. Ashford and ?

TWO OF US No.3

Answers

1. Lee.
2. Peoples.
3. Paula.
4. Olivia Newton-John.
5. Dec.
6. Duncan (aka Ant and Dec).
7. Jack.
8. Pace.
9. Renato.
10. Yvette .... but could also be Angela.
11. DJ E-Z Rock.
12. Kim (either the Appleby's or Mel Smith and Kim Wilde!).
13. Yvonne Keeley.
14. DeeDee.
15. Michael.
16. Womack.
17. Marcia ..... but could also be 'Earl'.
18. Spurling ..... but could also be 'James'.
19. The Boyz.
20. Simpson.

BLANK SPACE No.7

Fill in the blanks to reveal bands that have had chart hits:

1. G _ O _ O _ D _ L _ S
2. C _ O _ N _ E _ G _ T _ A _ F _ I _
3. C _ U _ T _ N _ C _ O _ S
4. E _ R _ H _ I _ D _ N _ F _ R _
5. J _ F _ E _ S _ N _ I _ P _ A _ E
6. H _ N _ Y _ O _ B _
7. G _ R _ L _ A _
8. P _ A _ N _ H _ T _ T _
9. F _ I _ P _ R _ C _ N _ E _ T _ O _
10. L _ V _ A _ F _ I _
11. T _ O _ P _ O _ T _ I _ S
12. G _ I _ T _ R _ A _ D
13. F _ U _ T _ I _ S _ F _ A _ N _
14. V _ L _ A _ E _ E _ P _ E
15. C _ A _ Y _ O _ L _ O _ A _ T _ U _ B _ O _ N
16. H _ T _ E _ S
17. A _ O _ L _ F _ U _ F _ R _ Y
18. B _ A _ K _ R _ P _
19. C _ A _ T _ O _ O _ S _
20. C _ Y _ E _ A _ L _ Y _ T _ M _ E _ S

BLANK SPACE No.7

ANSWERS

1. Goo Goo Dolls.
2. Crown Heights Affair.
3. Counting Crows.
4. Earth Wind and Fire.
5. Jefferson Airplane.
6. Honeycombs.
7. Gorillaz.
8. Plain White T's.
9. Fairport Convention.
10. Love Affair.
11. Thompson Twins.
12. Glitter Band.
13. Fountains of Wayne.
14. Village People.
15. Crazy World of Arthur Brown.
16. Hotlegs.
17. Apollo Four Forty.
18. Black Grape.
19. Coast to Coast.
20. Clyde Valley Stompers.

LIVIN' THING No.3

Which creatures are missing from these song titles?

1   I am the _ _ _ _ _ _ (The Beatles)
2   _ _ _ _ for the _ _ _ _ _ _ (Malcolm McLaren)
3   _ _ _ _ _ in a spotlight (Emerson Lake and Palmer)
4   The _ _ _ _ sleeps tonight (Tight Fit)
5   Little red _ _ _ _ _ _ _ (Rolling Stones)
6   _ _ _ _ _ _ _ _ _ (Jonathan Richman)
7   A message to Martha (Kentucky _ _ _ _ _ _ _ _) (Adam Faith)
8   _ _ _ _ _ _ _   _ _ _ _ (Frankie Laine)
9   A _ _ _ _ _ with no name (America)
10 Poor _ _ _ (Donovan)
11 What's new _ _ _ _ _ _ _ _ ? (Tom Jones)
12 Hey _ _ _ _ _ _ _ _ (The Beatles)
13 _ _ _ _ _ feet (Mud)
14 The _ _ _ _ _ _ _ (Mastodon)
15 _ _ _ _ _ _ (Chas and Dave)
16 The love _ _ _ _ (The Cure)
17 _ _ _ of war (AC/DC)
18 Running _ _ _ _ (Johnny Preston)
19 _ _ _ _ _ _ _ _ _ on a wheel (Mission)
20 The _ _ _ _ _ song (David Cassidy).

LIVIN' THING No.3

Answers

1 Walrus.
2 Duck, Oyster.
3 Tiger.
4 Lion.
5 Rooster.
6 Roadrunner.
7 Bluebird.
8 Humming Bird.
9 Horse.
10 Cow.
11 Pussycat.
12 Bulldog.
13 Tiger.
14 Sparrow.
15 Rabbit.
16 Cats.
17 Dogs.
18 Bear.
19 Butterfly.
20 Puppy.

ALL SHOOK UP No.4

Can you unravel the anagrams to identify these music personalities?

1. RUIN ALANA GRAB
2. LAMB CLAP LIE
3. RUIN A LATE BIG MAIL
4. BE BIT WARM
5. NOT LAND TARDIS
6. ROARS SPAM
7. PULL BIT
8. ON A VERY FIN
9. SOME KID BROTHER
10. CANVEY JO
11. SO CREW RHYL
12. BOB YULE
13. LOCK IN GEAR
14. BANKED LAURA REX
15. LACK BIKER
16. I TRY SUN BREW
17. SOUR WALL
18. VANE AS SIN
19. VILLA IS LOW
20. RIP RUN SCARES PESTS

ALL SHOOK UP No.4

Answers

1. LAURA BRANIGAN
2. ALI CAMPBELL
3. NATALIE IMBRUGLIA
4. MARTI WEBB
5. LINDA RONSTADT
6. SAM SPARRO
7. PITBULL
8. YVONNE FAIR
9. MEREDITH BROOKS
10. VANCE JOY
11. SHERYL CROW
12. BLUE BOY
13. CAROLE KING
14. ALEXANDRA BURKE
15. ACKER BILK
16. RUBY WINTERS
17. LOU RAWLS
18. SIAN EVANS
19. VIOLA WILLS
20. PRINCESS SUPERSTAR

LUCKY NUMBER No.4

Which cardinal or ordinal numbers are missing from these song titles?

1   Stars over _____ (Chas and Dave)

2   _____ letters (Take That)

3   Looking after No. _____ (Boomtown Rats)

4   _____ - _____ - _____ O'Leary (Des O'Connor)

5   Disco _____ (Pulp)

6   _____ wheeler (Pink)

7   _____ (Metallica)

8   _____ love (Adele)

9   It takes _____ (Marvin Gaye and Kim Weston)

10   _____ tears (Goombay Dance Band)

11   I'm Henry the _____ , I am (Herman's Hermits)

12   _____ steps to heaven (Eddie Cochran)

13   Grade _____ (Ed Sheeran)

14   _____ legit _____ quit (Hammer)

15   _____ crash (Suzi Quatro)

16   _____ son (Georgie Fame)

17   I'm gonna be (_____ miles) (Proclaimers)

18   _____ light years from home (Rolling Stones)

19   _____ (Paul Hardcastle)

20   _____ times a lady (Commodores)

LUCKY NUMBER No.4

Answers

1	Forty five.
2	Eight.
3	One.
4	One, Two, Three.
5	Two thousand.
6	Eighteen.
7	One.
8	First.
9	Two.
10	Seven.
11	Eighth.
12	Three.
13	Eight.
14	Two, two.
15	Forty eight.
16	Seventh.
17	Five hundred.
18	Two thousand.
19	Nineteen.
20	Three.

THERE'S A PLACE No.4

Which place name is missing from these song titles?

1   Going to _____ (Led Zeppelin)

2   Sun of _____ (Goombay Dance Band)

3   _____ cathedral (New Vaudeville Band)

4   _____ boy (Don Fardon)

5   Sweet _____ Brown (Ray Charles)

6   _____ rain (Elvis Presley)

7   Bagpipes from _____ (Eminem)

8   _____ (Freddie Mercury and Monserrat Caballe)

9   _____ (Marty Wilde)

10   The night _____ died (Paper Lace)

11   ____ rifles (The Jam)

12   _____ dock (Pink Floyd)

13   Kids in _____ (Kim Wilde)

14   _____ Joe (Bryan Ferry)

15   The _____ waltz (Vera Lynn)

16   _____ girls (Chas and Dave)

17   _____ (George Ezra)

18   _____ (Hole)

19   _____ (Mike Oldfield)

20   _____ (Perry Como)

THERE'S A PLACE No.4

Answers

1	California.
2	Jamaica.
3	Winchester.
4	Belfast.
5	Georgia.
6	Kentucky.
7	Baghdad.
8	Barcelona.
9	Abergavenny.
10	Chicago.
11	Eton.
12	Southampton.
13	America.
14	Tokyo.
15	Windsor.
16	London.
17	Budapest.
18	Malibu.
19	Portsmouth.
20	Delaware.

EMPTY SPACES No.8

Fill in the blanks to reveal musicians who have had chart hits:

1. K _ M   _ P _ L _ B _
2. B _ R _ Y   _ I _ G _
3. N _ T _ L _ E   _ O _ E
4. B _ N _   C _ O _ B _
5. L _ U _ A   _ R _ N _ G _ N
6. M _ R _ E _ L _   D _ T _ O _ T
7. H _ M _ L _ O _   B _ H _ N _ N
8. V _ O _ A   _ I _ L _
9. R _ C _ A _ D   _ L _ C _ W _ O _
10. A _ R _ L   _ A _ I _ N _
11. G _ O _ G _   E _ R _
12. C _ M _ L _   C _ B _ L _ O
13. T _ N _   B _ A _ T _ N
14. S _ G _ R   M _ N _ T _
15. B _ T _ E   _ I _ D _ E _
16. S _ O _ A   _ M _
17. K _ A _ A   _ E _ T _ E
18. G _ A _ A _   B _ N _ E _
19. C _ N _ I _   F _ A _ C _ S
20. C _ U _ B _   C _ E _ K _ R

EMPTY SPACES No.8

ANSWERS

1. Kim Appleby.
2. Barry Biggs.
3. Natalie Cole.
4. Bing Crosby.
5. Laura Branigan.
6. Marcella Detroit.
7. Hamilton Bohannon.
8. Viola Wills.
9. Richard Blackwood.
10. Avril Lavigne.
11. George Ezra.
12. Camila Cabello.
13. Toni Braxton.
14. Sugar Minott.
15. Bette Middler.
16. Shola Ama.
17. Keala Settle.
18. Graham Bonnet.
19. Connie Francis.
20. Chubby Checker.

THE NAME GAME No.7

By what names are the following better known:

1. Douglas Trendle.
2. Cherilyn Sarkisian.
3. William George Perks.
4. Florian Cloud de Bounevialle Armstrong.
5. Colin David Tooley.
6. Richard Maxwell.
7. Farrokh Bulsara.
8. Thomas DeCarlo Burton.
9. Ronald Wycherley.
10. Cornell Iral Haynes.
11. Vincent Eugene Craddock.
12. Armando Christian Perez.
13. Katherine Laverne Starks.
14. Robert Allen Zimmerman.
15. Frederick Albert Heath.
16. Austin Richard Post.
17. Francesco Stephen Castelluccio.
18. Anna Mae Bullock.
19. Albert George Cernik.
20. Elizabeth Woodridge Grant.

THE NAME GAME No.7

Answers

1. Buster Bloodvessel.
2. Cher.
3. Bill Wyman.
4. Dido.
5. Carl Wayne.
6. Dickie Valentine.
7. Freddie Mercury.
8. CeeLo Green.
9. Billy Fury.
10. Nelly.
11 Gene Vincent.
12. Pitbull.
13. Kay Starr.
14. Bob Dylan.
15. Johnny Kidd.
16. Post Malone.
17. Frankie Valli.
18. Tina Turner.
19. Guy Mitchell.
20. Lana Del Rey.

WORDS No.7

Can you identify these famous songs from their opening lyrics:

1. Talking away. I don't know what I'm to say. I'll say it anyway. Today's another day ...
2. Oh yeah, yeah, yeah. Now if there's a smile upon my face. It's only there trying to fool the public ....
3. Don't want your love anymore. Don't want your kisses that's for sure ....
4. My life is brilliant. My life is brilliant. My love is pure. I saw an angel ....
5. I never saw it as the start. It's more a change of heart. Rapping on the windows ....
6. Travelling in a fried-out Kombi, on a hippie trail full of zombie . ...
7. This was never the way I planned. Not my intention. I got so brave, drink in hand .....
8. They seek him here, they seek him there. His clothes are loud, but never square .....
9. Oh, we were born within an hour of each other. Our mothers said we could be sister and brother ....
10. Listen to the ground: There is movement all around. There is something goin' down ...
11. Looking fom a window above, it's like a story of love. Can you hear me? ....
12. Every night, I remember that evening. The way you looked when you said you were leaving ....
13. Oh yeah, I'll tell you something I think you'll understand. When I say that .....
14. Help me escape this feelin' of insecurity. I need you so much ....
15. We'll be fighting in the streets, with our children at our feet. And the morals that they worship will be gone ...
16. We're no strangers to love. You know the rules and so do I. A full commitment's ....
17. Na na na na na na. I guess I just lost my husband, I don't know where he went .....
18. Trailer for sale or rent. Room to let fifty cents. No phone, no pool, no pets ....
19. Ah well, here we are and here we are and here we go. All aboard and we're hitting the road ....
20. After love, after love. No matter how hard I try, you keep pushing me aside ....

WORDS No.7

Answers

1. Take on me (Aha).
2. The tears of a clown (Smokey Robinson).
3. Cathy's clown (Everly Brothers).
4. You're beautiful (James Blunt).
5. The day we caught the train (Ocean Colour Scene).
6. Down under (Men at Work).
7. I kissed a girl (Katie Perry).
8. Dedicated follower of fashion (The Kinks).
9. Disco 2000 (Pulp).
10. Night fever (Bee Gees).
11. Only you (Yazoo).
12. This ain't a love song (Scouting for Girls).
13. I want to hold your hand (The Beatles).
14. Relight my fire (Take That with Lulu).
15. Won't get fooled again (The Who).
16. Never gonna give you up (Rick Astley).
17. So what (Pink).
18. King of the road (Roger Miller).
19. Rockin' all over the world (Status Quo).
20. Believe (Cher).

COMMON PEOPLE No.3

What do the following have in common?

1. Ring ring, Voulez-vous, The visitors, Arrival, Super Trouper.

2. Frankie Bridge, Una Healey, Vanessa White, Rochelle Humes, Mollie King.

3. Laughing stock, The colour of spring, It's my life, Spirit of Eden, The party's over.

4. Peter Svensson, Bengt Lagerberg, Lars-Olof Johansson, Nina Persson, Magnus Sveningsson.

5. Sale of the century, Romeo me, She's a good girl, Inbetweener, Statuesque..

6. Neil Finn, Matt Sherrod, Nick Seymour, Craig Hooper, Paul Hester.

7. Trilogy, Pictures at an exhibition, Love beach, Tarkus, Brain salad surgery.

8. Nicki Minaj, Eminem, Maroon 5, Calvin Harris, Shakira.

9. Beauty on the fire, Big mistake, Shiver, Wrong impression, That day.

10. All the love in the world, Immortality, How deep is your love, Islands in the stream, Night of my life.

11. Pin ups, Lodger, Station to station, Earthling, Hunky dory.

12. Doesn't mean anything, No one, Girl on fire, You don't know my name, Girlfriend

13. Concrete and clay, Go now, Long live love, Make it easy on yourself, I'm alive.

14. Wired to the moon, King of the beach, Shamrock diaries, God's great banana skin, Dancing down the stony road.

15. Las Ketchup, Zager and Evans, Charlene, Lily Wood, MARRS.

16. Mike Ogletree, Ged Grimes, Brian McGee, Derek Forbes, Gordie Goudie.

17. Sunrise, Don't know why, Chasing pirates, Come away with me, Feelin' the same way.

18. Eric Clapton, Peter Green, Aynsley Dunbar, Andy Fraser, Mick Taylor.

19. Resistance is futile, Postcards from a young man, Gold against the soul, Everything must go, Send away the tigers.

20. Maddy Prior, Graham Nash, Colleen Nolan, Chris Lowe, Nick McCarthy.

COMMON PEOPLE No.3

ANSWERS

1. They are all albums by Abba.
2. They are The Saturdays.
3. They are all albums by Talk Talk.
4. They are the Cardigans.
5. They are all hit singles by 'Sleeper'.
6. They were all members of Crowded House.
7. They are all albums by Emerson Lake and Palmer.
8. They have all had hits featuring Rihanna.
9. They were all hit singles by Natalie Imbruglia.
10. They were all written (or co-written) by Barry Gibb.
11. They are all albums by David Bowie.
12. They are all hit singles by Alicia Keys.
13. They were all No.1 hits from 1965.
14. They were all albums by Chris Rea.
15. They all reached No.1 with their one and only hit single.
16. They were all members of 'Simple Minds'.
17. They were all hit singles by Nora Jones.
18. They were all members of John Mayall's Bluesbreakers.
19. They are all albums by Manic Street Preachers.
20. They were all born in Blackpool.

WHO ARE YOU? No.7

Which name is missing from these song titles?

1.   _ _ _ _ _ _ (Four Seasons)

2.   Sweet _ _ _ _ _ _ _ Brown (Ray Charles)

3.   _ _ _ _ _ don't lose that number (Steely Dan)

4.   Not now _ _ _ _ (Pink Floyd)

5.   _ _ _ _   _ _ _ _ (Megadeath)

6.   Tokyo _ _ _ (Bryan Ferry)

7.   _ _ _ _ _ _ _ _   _ _ _ _ _ _ Bell (Sweet)

8.   _ _ _ _ _ _ _ 's silver hammer (The Beatles)

9.   Gimme hope _ _ _ _ _ _ (Eddy Grant)

10. _ _ _ _ _ (Gilbert O'Sullivan)

11. Just like _ _ _ _ (Heinz)

12. _ _ _ _ _   _ _ _ _ (Kenny)

13. Bring a little water, _ _ _ _ _ _ (Lonnie Donegan)

14. _ _ _ _ _ can move mountains (Johnny Rae)

15. The day that curly _ _ _ _ _ shot down crazy _ _ _ McGee (The Hollies)

16. _ _ _ _ _ _ _ honey (Tommy Roe)

17. Hurry up _ _ _ _ _ (Sham 69)

18. Black pudding _ _ _ _ _ _ (Goodies)

19. _ _ _ _ _ 's house (Eels)

20. _ _ _ _   _ _ _ _ (The Shadows)

WHO ARE YOU? No.7

Answers

1   Sherry.
2   Georgia.
3   Rikki.
4   John.
5   Mary Jane.
6   Joe.
7   Alexander, Graham.
8   Maxwell.
9   Jo'anna.
10 Clair.
11 Eddy.
12 Julie Anne.
13 Sylvie.
14 Faith.
15 Billy, Sam.
16 Heather.
17 Harry.
18 Bertha.
19 Susan.
20 Mary Anne.

JOIN TOGETHER No.4

These groups were known for backing which musician?

1. The Pirates.
2. The Modern Lovers.
3. The MG's.
4. The Blue Notes.
5. The Bruvvers.
6. The Dipsticks.
7. His Spirit of Life.
8. The FBI.
9. The Bandwagon.
10. The Hurricanes.
11. The Marksmen.
12. Wings.
13. The Stingers.
14. The Family Cookin'.
15. The Plastic Population.
16. The Bunnymen.
17. Dawn.
18. The Jumping Jacks.
19. The Mysterians.
20. The Checkmates.

JOIN TOGETHER No.4

Answers

1. Johnny Kidd.
2. Jonathan Richman.
3. Booker T.
4. Harold Melvin.
5. Joe Brown.
6. Laurie Lingo (Dave Lee Travis and Paul Burnett).
7. David Devant.
8. Redhead Kingpin.
9. Johnny Johnston.
10. Johnny (Paris).
11. Houston Wells.
12. Paul McCartney.
13. B Bumble.
14. Limmie (Snell).
15. Yazz.
16. Echo.
17. Tony Orlando.
18. Danny Peppermint.
19. ? (Question Mark).
20. Emile Ford.

BLANK SPACE No.8

Fill in the blanks to reveal bands that have had chart hits:

1. A _ T _ F _ O _ S _
2. B _ G _ O _ N _ R _
3. Z _ G _ R _ N _ E _ A _ S
4. B _ B _ S _ A _ B _ E _
5. B _ R _ L _ Y _ A _ E _ H _ R _ E _ T
6. S _ U _ S _ E _ E _ Z
7. T _ U _ D _ R _ L _ P _ E _ M _ N
8. B _ S _ T _ P
9. M _ D _ L _ O _ T _ E _ O _ D
10. T _ N _ I _ O _ T
11. S _ A _ E _ P _ A _ S _ I _ T _ R
12. J _ M _ R _ Q _ A _
13. D _ E _ M _ _ C _ D _ M _
14. B _ L _ E _ _ T _ R _
15. D _ F _ P _ N _
16. C _ L _ R _ E _ A _ D
17. T _ A _ F _ C
18. E _ H _ B _ L _ Y
19. S _ R _ Y _ A _ S
20. Y _ R _ R _ U _ H _ N _ P _ O _ L _ S

BLANK SPACE No.8

ANSWERS

1. Art of Noise.
2. Big Country.
3. Zager and Evans.
4. Babyshambles.
5. Barclay James Harvest.
6. Soul Seekerz.
7. Thunderclap Newman.
8. Bus Stop.
9. Middle of the Road.
10. Tin Tin Out.
11. Shakespears Sister.
12. Jamiroquai.
13. Dream Academy.
14. Belle Stars.
15. Daft Punk.
16. Color Me Badd.
17. Traffic.
18. Echobelly.
19. Stray Cats.
20. Yarbrough and Peoples.

WOULD I LIE TO YOU? No.4

Are the following statements true or false?

1. 'Happy', 'Trust', 'Stuck' and 'Intact' were all hit singles by Ned's Atomic Dustbin.

2. Groovejet (if this ain't love) was a No.1 hit for Sophie Ellis Bextor with Spiller.

3. Lena Zavaroni is the youngest person to have a UK No.1 album.

4. Jonathan King was the person behind 'Bubblerock', 'The Weathermen' and 'Sakkarin'.

5. Esther Ofarim represented Israel in the Eurovision Song Contest.

6. Hilda and Rob Woodward of Lieutenant Pigeon are the only mother and son to feature on a No.1 hit.

7. Carol Decker was the lead singer with 'T'Pau'.

8. Both Oasis and Mike Flowers Pops reached No.1 in the charts in 1996 with 'Wonderwall'.

9. David van Day and Thereza Bazar were in both 'Brotherhood of Man' and 'Dollar'.

10. Susan Brice is professionally known as Coco Pops.

11. Richie Spice, Snatcha Lion, Pliers and Spanner Banner are all brothers.

12. Robin Sarstedt, Peter Sarstedt and Eden Kane were all brothers.

13. Bob Marley was born in Kingston, Jamaica in 1943.

14. 'Young girl' was the only UK chart hit for the Union Gap featuring Gary Puckett.

15. Systems in Blue, Electric Light Orchestra and Debbie Gibson have all recorded an album called 'Out of the blue'..

16. The New Seekers, Marty Kristian, was born as Martins Vanags in Amsterdam, Netherlands.

17. Linda Ronstadt started her recording career as lead singer with The Stone Poneys.

18. Doris Day had almost 10 hits in the USA before having a chart hit in the UK.

19. Ward Thomas consists of twins Catherine and Lizzy Ward Thomas.

20. Brandon Flowers was lead singer with The Killers.

WOULD I LIE TO YOU? No.4

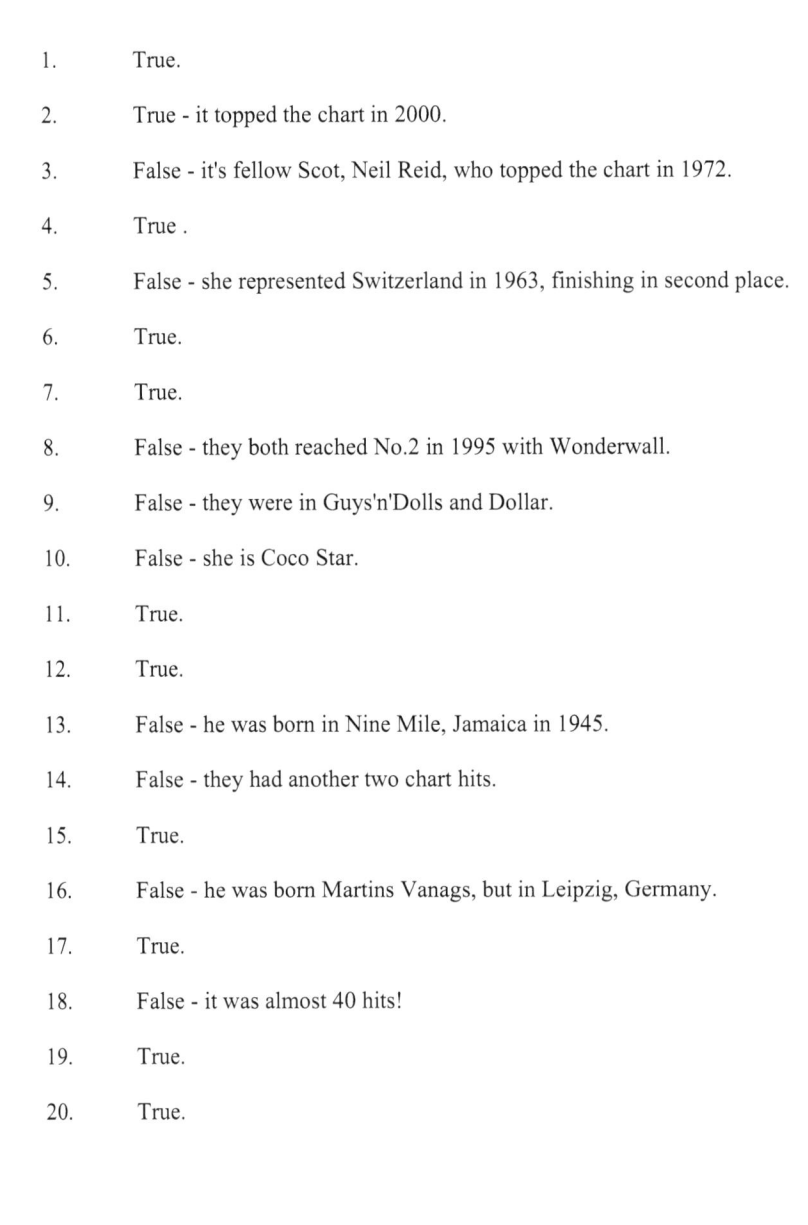

Answers

1. True.
2. True - it topped the chart in 2000.
3. False - it's fellow Scot, Neil Reid, who topped the chart in 1972.
4. True .
5. False - she represented Switzerland in 1963, finishing in second place.
6. True.
7. True.
8. False - they both reached No.2 in 1995 with Wonderwall.
9. False - they were in Guys'n'Dolls and Dollar.
10. False - she is Coco Star.
11. True.
12. True.
13. False - he was born in Nine Mile, Jamaica in 1945.
14. False - they had another two chart hits.
15. True.
16. False - he was born Martins Vanags, but in Leipzig, Germany.
17. True.
18. False - it was almost 40 hits!
19. True.
20. True.

HAPPY BIRTHDAY No.5

Can you identify these musicians?

1. Singer born in Lafayette, Indiana, USA on 6 February 1962.
2. Singer and TV presenter born in Kingston upon Thames, England on 22 Sept 1953.
3. Singer born in Victoria, Canada on 2 December 1978.
4. Singer and drummer born in London, England on 30 January1951.
5. Bassist born in Tredegar, Wales on 20 January 1969.
6. Singer born in Eureka, California, USA on 7 December 1979.
7. Singer and guitarist born in Glasgow, Scotland on 12 August 1949.
8. Singer born in Redditch, England on 9 February 1994.
9. Rapper born in Atlanta, USA on 8 June 1977.
10. Singer born in Bjorkasen, Norway on 15 November 1945.
11. Guitarist born in Autlan de Navarro, Mexico on 20 July 1947.
12. Singer born in Reykjavik, Iceland on 21 November 1965.
13. Singer born in Leeds, England on 29 May 1975.
14. Singer born in Cleveland, USA on 30 March 1964.
15. Singer born in Clydebank, Scotland on 23 March 1965.
16. Guitarist born in Belfast, Northern Ireland on 4 April 1952.
17. Singer and guitarist born in Kingston, Canada on 5 November 1959.
18. Singer born in Cardiff, Wales on 11 April 1969.
19. Singer and pianist born in Pinner, England on 25 March 1947.
20. Singer born in Sydney, Australia on 8 November 1982.

HAPPY BIRTHDAY No.5

Answers

1. Axl Rose.
2. Richard Fairbrass.
3. Nelly Furtado.
4. Phil Collins.
5. Nicky Wire.
6. Sara Bareilles.
7. Mark Knopfler.
8. Harry Styles.
9. Kanye West.
10. Anni-Frid Lyngstad.
11. Carlos Santana.
12. Bjork.
13. Mel B.
14. Tracy Chapman.
15. Marti Pellow.
16. Gary Moore.
17. Bryan Adams.
18. Cerys Matthews.
19. Elton John.
20. Sam Sparro.

MIX IT UP No.5

Can you unravel the anagrams to identify these hit making bands?

1. OR CHEATS HER CLIMB
2. SMASH BY BABEL
3. EDAM MADE A CRY
4. HELL BE COY
5. TREBLE LASS
6. SET FAR YET NEAR
7. USED LOLA
8. TELL US COVER UP
9. IN NICE TRY
10. METAL BRATS
11. KEY LIDO JUG
12. VEER OUT IN ECO
13. QUILL DID GO
14. A LOUSY SLUM
15. ABLE SET
16. TOSSER NOSE
17. OK NEW SLY MOB
18. MY LINK HAD ONE
19. A RAG ROOM DAVE
20. ROSE AS SHE

MIX IT UP No.5

Answers

1. CHEMICAL BROTHERS
2. BABYSHAMBLES
3. DREAM ACADEMY
4. ECHOBELLY
5. BELLE STARS
6. TEN YEARS AFTER
7. DE LA SOUL
8. LOVE SCULPTURE
9. INNER CITY
10. LAMBRETTAS
11. UGLY KID JOE
12. ONE TRUE VOICE
13. LIQUID GOLD
14. SOUL ASYLUM
15. BEATLES
16. STONE ROSES
17. BLOW MONKEYS
18. MILK AND HONEY
19. GROOVE ARMADA
20. SEAHORSES

WHO ARE YOU? No.8

Which name is missing from these song titles?

1. _ _ _ _ _ _ (Tommy Roe)
2. _ _ _ _ _ don't you grieve (Lonnie Donegan)
3. My girl _ _ _ _ _ _ _ _ _ (Fats Domino)
4. Little _ _ _ _ _ (The Sweet)
5. _ _ _ _ _ _ my dear (The Beatles)
6. There's a guy works down the chip shop swears he's _ _ _ _ _ (Kirsty MacColl)
7. _ _ _ _ _ _ _ _ _ (Everly Brothers)
8. _ _ _ _ _ _ _ the midget (the queen of the blues) (Ray Stevens)
9. _ _ _ _ _ _ _ _ (P J Harvey)
10. _ _ _ _ _ _ 99 (Bruce Springsteen)
11. _ _ _ _ _ _ girl (The Seekers)
12. Lay down _ _ _ _ _ (Eric Clapton)
13. _ _ _ _ _ (Cilla Black)
14. Sister _ _ _ _ (New World)
15. _ _ _ _ _ Smith and his amazing dancing bear (Alan Price)
16. My friend _ _ _ _ (Slade)
17. Lady _ _ _ _ _ _ _ (Herman's Hermits)
18. Help me, _ _ _ _ _ _ (Beach Boys)
19. _ _ _ _ _ _ _ _ _ _ (Thunderclap Newman)
20. _ _ _ _ _ _ Bender (Emerson Lake and Palmer)

WHO ARE YOU? No.8

Answers

1   Sheila.
2   Sally.
3   Josephine.
4   Willy.
5   Martha.
6   Elvis.
7   Claudette.
8   Bridget.
9   Henry, Lee.
10 Johnny.
11 Georgy.
12 Sally.
13 Alfie.
14 Jane.
15 Simon.
16 Stan.
17 Barbara.
18 Rhonda.
19 Wilhelmina.
20 Jeremy.

EMPTY SPACES No.9

Fill in the blanks to reveal musicians who have had chart hits:

1. P _ U _ O   _ H _ R _ I _ G _ O _
2. P _ G _ Y   _ E _
3. B _ L _ Y   _ W _ N
4. T _ M _ Y   _ Y _ E _ T _
5. D _ S _ O _ D   _ E _ K _ R
6. C _ R _ S _ I _ A   _ G _ I _ E _ R _
7. P _ U _   C _ R _ A _ K
8. K _ T _   B _ S _
9. A _ M _   C _ G _ N
10. G _ E _   S _ E _ A _ I
11. D _ N _ E _   P _ W _ E _
12. J _ D _   C _ L _ I _ S
13. A _ H _ N _ I
14. D _ A _   M _ R _ I _
15. N _ L _ Y   _ U _ T _ D _
16. B _ L _ Y   _ A _ L
17. C _ A _ L _ T _ E   _ H _ R _ H
18. J _ S _   J _ C _
19. E _ A _ N _   P _ I _ E
20. P _ P _   R _ A _ H

EMPTY SPACES No.9

ANSWERS

1. Pluto Shervington.
2. Peggy Lee.
3. Billy Swan.
4. Tammy Wynette.
5. Desmond Dekker.
6. Christina Aguilera.
7. Paul Carrack.
8. Kate Bush.
9. Alma Cogan.
10. Gwen Stefani.
11. Daniel Powter.
12. Judy Collins.
13. Ashanti.
14. Dean Martin.
15. Nelly Furtado.
16. Billy Paul.
17. Charlotte Church.
18. Just Jack.
19. Elaine Paige.
20. Papa Roach.

WORDS No.8

Can you identify these famous songs from their opening lyrics:

1. Just a small town girl livin' in a lonely world. She took the midnight train ...

2. She keeps Moet et Chandon in her pretty cabinet. 'Let them eat cake' she says ....

3. Bed, stay in bed. The feeling of your skin locked in my head. Smoke ....

4. It's automatic when I talk with old friends, the conversation turns to girls we knew ....

5. I've known a few guys who thought they were pretty smart. But you've got being right down to an art ....

6. I met her in a club down in old Soho, where you drink champagne . ...

7. Even when you're home, you won't pick up your phone and take my call .....

8. I thought I saw a man brought to life. He was warm, he came around .....

9. When I was a little girl I had a rag doll. Only doll I've ever owned ....

10. 'Oh don't you dare look back, just keep your eyes on me' I said you're holding back ....

11. Summer in the city where the air is still. A baby being born to the overkill ....

12. I don't care if Monday's blue, Tuesday's grey and Wednesday too ....

13. I've been walkin' these streets so long, singin' the same old song .....

14. One, two, three o'clock, four o'clock rock. Five, six, seven o'clock ....

15. You say you wander your own land. But when I think about it, I don't see how you can ...

16. Do you remember a guy that's been in such an early song? I've heard a rumour ....

17. I saw the light on the night that I passed by her window .....

18. (Morning! Today's forecast calls for blue skies) Sun is shining in the sky ....

19. All the times I have laid in your light, when your love kept me safe ....

20. Is it my imagination, or have I finally found something worth living for? ....

WORDS No.8

Answers

1. Don't stop believin' (Journey).
2. Killer Queen (Queen).
3. Talking body (Tove Lo).
4. Do it again (Beach Boys).
5. That don't impress me much (Shania Twain).
6. Lola (The Kinks).
7. You'll never stop me loving you (Sonia).
8. Torn (Natalie Imbruglia).
9. River deep mountain high (Ike and Tina Turner).
10. Shut up and dance (Walk The Moon).
11. Somewhere in my heart (Aztec Camera).
12. Friday I'm in love (The Cure).
13. Rhinestone cowboy (Glen Campbell).
14. Rock around the clock (Bill Haley).
15. Everybody's changing (Keane).
16. Ashes to ashes (David Bowie).
17. Delilah (Tom Jones).
18. Mr Blue Sky (Electric Light Orchestra).
19. Lullaby (Professor Green with Tori Kelly).
20. Cigarettes and alcohol (Oasis).

THE NAME GAME No.8

By what names are the following better known:

1. Thomas Gregory Jackson.
2. James Curtis Jackson.
3. Yasmine Evans.
4. Rudy Martinez.
5. Richard Melville Hall.
6. Karla Estrabo.
7. Joscelyn Eve Stoker.
8. Antonio Carmine Di Bartolomeo.
9. Michael Emile Telford Miller.
10. Robert Matthew Van Winkle.
11. Caroline Esmerelda van der Leeuw.
12. Geethali Shankar.
13. Peter Slaghuis.
14. Donald Arthur Maughn.
15. Maxwell Fraser.
16. Ayalah Deborah Bentovim.
17. Michael Cassavitis.
18. Henry Olusegun Adeola Samuel.
19. Eva Narcissus Boyd.
20. Christopher Edwin Breaux.

THE NAME GAME No.8

Answers

1. Tommy James.
2. 50 Cent.
3. Yazz.
4. ? (Question Mark).
5. Moby.
6. Camila Cabello ..... and these are her middle names, that we left out!
7. Joss Stone.
8. Tony Di Bart.
9. Emile Ford.
10. Vanilla Ice.
11 Caro Emerald.
12. Nora Jones (her middle names are Nora Jones!).
13. Hithouse.
14. Don Fardon.
15. Maxi Jazz.
16. Sister Bliss.
17. Tony Orlando (his middle names are Anthony Orlando).
18. Seal.
19. Little Eva.
20. Frank Ocean.

ANY COLOUR YOU LIKE No.3

Which colour is missing from these song titles?

1   Lil' _____ Riding Hood (Sam the Sham)

2   _____ city (The Seekers)

3   _____ haze (Jimi Hendrix)

4   Big _____ taxi (Joni Mitchell)

5   Paint it _____ (Rolling Stones)

6   Song sung _____ (Neil Diamond)

7   _____ (Led Zeppelin)

8   _____ (Aerosmith)

9   Heart of _____ (Neil Young)

10   Little _____ apples (Roger Miller)

11   The _____ balloon (Dave Clark Five)

12   _____ Monday (Fats Domino)

13   My _____ bicycle (Nazareth)

14   _____ eyed girl (Van Morrison)

15   Little _____ rooster (Rolling Stones)

16   _____ glove (Pulp)

17   _____ is the colour (Pink Floyd)

18   Deep _____ (Donny and Marie Osmond)

19   _____ (Hoobastank)

20   The court of the _____ King (King Crimson)

ANY COLOUR YOU LIKE No.3

Answers

1. Red.
2. Emerald.
3. Purple.
4. Yellow.
5. Black.
6. Blue.
7. Tangerine.
8. Pink.
9. Gold.
10. Green.
11. Red.
12. Blue.
13. White.
14. Brown.
15. Red.
16. Pink.
17. Green.
18. Purple.
19. Magnolia.
20. Crimson.

LUCKY NUMBER No.5

Which cardinal or ordinal numbers are missing from these song titles?

1   The _____ time ever I saw your face (Roberta Flack)
2   _____ little girls sitting in the backseat (The Avons)
3   _____ bars (Stylistics)
4   _____ stone from the sun (Jimi Hendrix)
5   Lucky _____ (Russ Conway)
6   _____ miles of bad road (Duane Eddy)
7   _____ days in the sun (Feeder)
8   A _____ pounds of clay (Craig Douglas)
9   _____ minutes (Missy 'Misdemeanor' Elliott)
10   _____ become _____ (Spice Girls)
11   _____ century man (Catherine Wheel)
12   Mr _____ class (Spencer Davis Group)
13   _____ disciple (Five Thirty)
14   _____ _____ (All Saints)
15   Free _____ (Pink Floyd)
16   Only _____ (Craig Douglas)
17   _____ (Iggy Azalia with Watch the Duck)
18   _____ yellow roses (Bobby Darin)
19   Just _____ numbers (can straighten out my life) (Four Tops)
20   _____ carats (Kelly Clarkson)

LUCKY NUMBER No.5

Answers

1   First.
2   Seven.
3   Sixteen.
4   Third.
5   Five.
6   Forty.
7   Seven.
8   Hundred.
9   Five.
10 Two, one.
11 Thirtieth.
12 Second.
13 Thirteenth.
14 Three, four.
15 Four.
16 Sixteen.
17 One hundred.
18 Eighteen.
19 Seven.
20 Four.

BLANK SPACE No.9

Fill in the blanks to reveal bands that have had chart hits:

1. T _ A _ D _ O _   E _ P _ O _ E _
2. S _ E _ L _ Y _   S _ A _
3. G _ D _ E _   A _ D   _ R _ M _
4. T _ D _ Y   _ E _ R _
5. B _ N _ N _ R _ M _   (*only one letter required!*)
6. A _ I _ E   _ E _ J _ Y
7. P _ A _ L   _ A _
8. G _ O _   C _ A _ L _ T _ E
9. M _ M _ N _ S   _ N _   W _ A _ N _ U _ S
10. L _ T _   F _ N _ I _   O _ E _
11. C _ O _ D _ D   _ O _ S _
12. V _ M _ I _ E   W _ E _ E _ D
13. F _ I _ H   _ O   _ O _ E
14. G _ E _ N   _ A _
15. C _ S _ I _   G _ T _
16. P _ R _ I _ H _ A _
17. S _ U _   A _ Y _ U _
18. P _ T _ R _   A _ D   _ E _
19. E _ E _ Y _ H _ N _   B _ T   _ H _   G _ R _
20. S _ I _ E _ L _ S

BLANK SPACE No.9

ANSWERS

1. Teardrop Explodes.
2. Steeleye Span.
3. Godley and Creme.
4. Teddy Bears.
5. Bananarama.
6. Alice DeeJay.
7. Pearl Jam.
8. Good Charlotte.
9. Moments and Whatnauts.
10. Lyte Funkie Ones.
11. Crowded House.
12. Vampire Weekend.
13. Faith No More.
14. Green Day.
15. Cosmic Gate.
16. Portishead.
17. Soul Asylum.
18. Peters and Lee.
19. Everything but the Girl.
20. Shirelles.

THERE'S A PLACE No.5

Which place name is missing from these song titles?

1 _ _ _ _ _ _ (Ultravox)

2 _ _ _ _ _ _ _ _ central (New Vaudeville Band)

3 A New _ _ _ _ _ _ _ (Kirsty MacColl)

4 _ _ _ _ _ _ (Malcolm McLaren)

5 The man from _ _ _ _ _ _ _ (Jimmy Young)

6 The man from _ _ _ _ _ _ _ _ (John Paul Joans)

7 _ _ _ _ _ _ _ song (David Bowie)

8 Asylums in _ _ _ _ _ _ _ _ _ (Scritti Politti)

9 _ _ _ _ _ _ _ (Sash!)

10 _ _ _ _ _ _ _ _ _ nights (Bob Seger)

11 Sunshine on _ _ _ _ _ (Proclaimers)

12 _ _ _ _ _ _ _ _ _ _ _ _ (Peter Gabriel)

13 _ _ _ _ _ _ _ _ (Bruce Springsteen)

14 Seven years in _ _ _ _ _ (David Bowie)

15 On a slow boat to _ _ _ _ _ (Emile Ford)

16 _ _ _ _ _ _ _ _ 'd in _ _ _ _ _ _ _ _ (Nazareth)

17 Back to _ _ _ _ _ _ _ _ _ (Billy Ray Cyrus)

18 _ _ _ _ _ _ _ _ (Oasis)

19 Day trip to _ _ _ _ _ _ (didn't we have a lovely time) (Fiddlers Dram)

20 _ _ _ _ _ _ city (Little Richard)

THERE'S A PLACE No.5

Answers

1	Vienna.
2	Finchley.
3	England.
4	Soweto.
5	Laramie.
6	Nazareth.
7	Alabama.
8	Jerusalem.
9	Ecuador.
10	Hollywood.
11	Leith.
12	Solsbury Hill.
13	Nebraska.
14	Tibet.
15	China.
16	Shanghai, Shanghai.
17	Tennessee.
18	Columbia.
19	Bangor.
20	Kansas.

ALL SHOOK UP No.5

Can you unravel the anagrams to identify these music personalities?

1. EAR MOTION
2. DRAWN MYRA RAVEN
3. DRY ALAN EEL
4. NEAR MAD NIT
5. I AM TWIT EARS
6. NICER SLY VODKA
7. ELLA ATE COIN
8. MONK WEAR
9. RID PUNK HOVEL
10. AH DAZE NELL
11. RAN MEAN JOG
12. CHINA AND A PIE
13. MILLY IS BEER
14. REAL WELL UP
15. SHAVE AND DROP
16. ANY AT A TAIL
17. A DRY AXLE BANKER
18. INK CRATE JET
19. PURILE HATCH
20. AN IRON HALL

ALL SHOOK UP No.5

Answers

1. TINA MOORE
2. RANDY VANWARMER
3. LANA DEL REY
4. DEAN MARTIN
5. AMII STEWART
6. VICKY LEANDROS
7. NATALIE COLE
8. MARK OWEN
9. KEVIN RUDOLPH
10. HAZELL DEAN
11. JANE MORGAN
12. APACHE INDIAN
13. BILLIE MYRES
14. PAUL WELLER
15. VONDA SHEPARD
16. TATYANA ALI
17. ALEXANDER RYBAK
18. JACKIE TRENT
19. CHARLIE PUTH
20. NIALL HORAN

LIVIN' THING No.4

Which creatures are missing from these song titles?

1	Little white _ _ _ _ (Tommy Steele)

2	_ _ _ _ _ _ _ (Aretha Franklin)

3	Union of the _ _ _ _ _ (Duran Duran)

4	I'm only a poor little _ _ _ _ _ _ _ (The Ramblers)

5	Me and you and a _ _ _ named Boo (Lobo)

6	White _ _ _ _ _ _ (Jefferson Airplane)

7	I go _ _ _ (Neil Sedaka)

8	The _ _ _ _ _ _ _ _ 's graveyard (Boomtown Rats)

9	_ _ _ on the run (Manfred Mann)

10	Ride a white _ _ _ _ (T Rex)

11	Mary had a little _ _ _ _ (Wings)

12	_ _ _ _ _ (Abba)

13	Paddy McGinty's _ _ _ _ (Val Doonican)

14	Diamond _ _ _ _ (David Bowie)

15	Peter Percival Patterson's pet _ _ _ porky (The Monkees)

16	Dark _ _ _ _ _ (George Harrison)

17	Little _ _ _ _ _ _ (Nina and Frederick)

18	Dig a _ _ _ _ (The Beatles)

19	Peter and the _ _ _ _ (Clyde Valley Stompers)

20	Them kinda _ _ _ _ _ _ _ can't swing (Slade)

LIVIN' THING No.4

Answers

1   Bull.
2   Skylark.
3   Snake.
4   Sparrow.
5   Dog.
6   Rabbit.
7   Ape.
8   Elephant.
9   Fox.
10   Swan.
11   Lamb.
12   Tiger ..... or Eagle.
13   Goat.
14   Dogs.
15   Pig.
16   Horse.
17   Donkey.
18   Pony.
19   Wolf.
20   Monkeys.

ABC No.2

The letters of the names of these groups have been arranged in alphabetical order. can you identify them?

1. DEEGHHINORTW.
2. BLNOOSSS.
3. BEEEHLORRRSTVY.
4. AABCEFGIILNNNNOSUY.
5. AADDEHIOR.
6. EILOPSSSTX.
7. BEEFHNORTUY.
8. ACEILMOPRRS.
9. EEEFIKLNNOSTUY.
10. ACE£HINOOOPRRSTU.
11. DMNOOSS.
12. AAILLNTSS.
13. ADDEEELOOPPRRSTX.
14. BDELMOOSUY.
15. AAEHJLMOS.
16. CDDEEEEHMOP.
17. ACEHILOOSSU.
18. ADIRWZZ.
19. AACEILLMT.
20. BEHOOPPSSTY.

ABC No.2

Answers

1. Eighth Wonder.
2. Blossoms.
3. Everly Brothers.
4. Fine Young Cannibals.
5. Radiohead.
6. Sex Pistols.
7. Fun Boy Three.
8. Proclaimers.
9. Lyte Funkie Ones.
10. Hues Corporation
11. Osmonds.
12. All Saints.
13. Teardrop Explodes.
14. Moddy Blues.
15. Halo James.
16. Depeche Mode.
17. Social House.
18. Wizzard.
19. Metallica.
20. Pet Shop Boys.

WHO ARE YOU? No.9

Which name is missing from these song titles?

1   Gudbuy T' _ _ _ _ (Slade)

2   So long, _ _ _ _ _   _ _ _ _ _ Wright (Simon and Garfunkel)

3   _ _ _ _ of the 4th form (Boomtown Rats)

4   Ave _ _ _ _ _ (Shirley Bassey)

5   _ _ _   _ _ _ turnaround (New World)

6   Goodbye _ _ _ hello _ _ _ _ _ _ _ _ (Cliff Richard)

7   The _ _ _ _ genie (David Bowie)

8   Yes tonight _ _ _ _ _ _ _ _ (Johnny Ray)

9   _ _ _ _ Wayne is big leggy (Haysi Fantayzee)

10   Dizzy, Miss _ _ _ _ _ (Larry Williams)

11   _ _ _ _ _ _ _ _ Eccles (The Hollies)

12   Are you ready, _ _ _ _ ? (Emerson Lake and Palmer)

13   _ _ _ _ _ _ _ _ (Abba)

14   _ _ _ _ _ _ is a punk rocker (Ramones)

15   Theme from ' _ _ _ _ _ 's Game' (Clannad)

16   _ _ _ _ _ _ _ (Don McLean)

17   _ _ _ _ _ boy (Daniel O'Donnell)

18   _ _ _ _ _ _ (Human League)

19   Goodnight _ _ _ _ _ (The Weavers)

20   _ _ _ _ and _ _ _ _ (Raydio)

WHO ARE YOU? No.9

Answers

1. Jane.
2. Frank, Lloyd.
3. Mary.
4. Maria.
5. Tom, Tom.
6. Sam, Samantha.
7. Jean.
8. Josephine.
9. John.
10. Lizzy.
11. Jennifer.
12. Eddy.
13. Fernando.
14. Sheena.
15. Harry.
16. Vincent.
17. Danny.
18. Louise.
19. Irene.
20. Jack, Jill.

WORDS No.9

Can you identify these famous songs from their opening lyrics:

1. It's a god awful-small affair to the girl with the mousy hair ....

2. Ever seen a blind man cross the road trying to make the other side? ....

3. I would lock you up, but I could not bear to hear you screaming to be set free ....

4. Woke up one morning half asleep, with all my blankets in a heap ....

5. You're the whisper of a summer breeze. You're the kiss that puts my soul at ease ....

6. When I find myself in times of trouble, mother Mary comes to me . ...

7. You say that we've got nothing in common. No common ground to start from.....

8. So you finally named the day when wedding bells will chime. I was sorry .....

9. Wrapped up, so consumed by all this hurt. If you ask me, don't know where to start ....

10. The Indians send signals from the rocks above the pass. The cowboys take position in the bushes and the grass ....

11. I didn't know what day it was when you walked in to the room. I said hello ....

12. Look at the stars. Look at how they shine for you and everything you do ....

13. Woke up this morning feelin' fine. There's something special on my mind .....

14. It's been seven hours and fifteen days since you took your love away ....

15. I hear the ticking of the clock. I'm lying here, the room's pitch dark ...

16. Look, if you had one shot, or one opportunity to seize everything ....

17. I looked out this morning and the sun was gone. Turned on some music .....

18. One night I was late, came home from a date. Slipped out of my shoes ....

19. I guess now it's time for me to give up. I feel it's time. Got a picture of you ....

20. Father wears his Sunday best. Mother's tired, she needs a rest. The kids are playing up downstairs ....

WORDS No.9

Answers

1. Life on Mars? (David Bowie).
2. Handbags and gladrags (Stereophonics).
3. The edge of Heaven (Wham!).
4. Flowers in the rain (The Move).
5. Rush rush (Paula Abdul).
6. Let it be (The Beatles).
7. Breakfast at Tiffany's (Deep Blue Something).
8. Semi detached suburban Mr James (Manfred Mann).
9. Take me home (Jess Glynne).
10. Cool for cats (Squeeze).
11. You're in my heart (the final acclaim) (Rod Stewart).
12. Yellow (Coldplay).
13. I'm into something good (Herman's Hermits).
14. Nothing compares 2 U (Sinead O'Connor).
15. Alone (Heart).
16. Lose yourself (Eminem).
17. More than a feeling (Boston).
18. Rock and roll waltz (Kay Starr).
19. Back for good (Take That).
20. Our house (Madness).

EMPTY SPACES No.10

Fill in the blanks to reveal musicians who have had chart hits:

1. S _ L _ N _   G _ M _ Z
2. G _ O _ G _   B _ N _ O _
3. K _ R _   D _ N _ E _
4. A _ I   _ A _ P _ E _ L
5. D _ V _ D   _ I _ M _ U _
6. J _ N _ T   _ A _ K _ O _
7. T _ N _   C _ A _ L _ S
8. S _ C _ A   _ I _ T _ L
9. J _ K _   G _ A _ A _
10. A _ R _ N   _ A _ T _ R
11. H _ Z _ L   _ C _ N _ O _
12. J _ Y _ E   _ I _ S
13. L _ T _ I _ I _   M _ N _ A _
14. Y _ O _ N _   E _ L _ M _ N
15. B _   D _ D _ L _ Y
16. C _ Y _ T _ L   _ A _ L _
17. H _ R _ L _   F _ L _ E _ M _ Y _ R
18. S _ A _ Y   _ A _ T _ S _ W
19. M _ R _ I   _ E _ B
20. S _ D _ E _   Y _ U _ G _ L _ O _

EMPTY SPACES No.10

ANSWERS

1. Selena Gomez.
2. George Benson.
3. Karl Denver.
4. Ali Campbell.
5. David Gilmour.
6. Janet Jackson.
7. Tina Charles.
8. Sacha Distel.
9. Jaki Graham.
10. Aaron Carter.
11. Hazel O'Connor.
12. Joyce Sims.
13. Lutricia McNeal.
14. Yvonne Elliman.
15. Bo Diddley.
16. Crystal Gayle.
17. Harold Faltermeyer.
18. Stacy Lattisaw.
19. Marti Webb.
20. Sydney Youngblood.

YOU'RE THE ONE No.3

Can you spot the odd one out in each case?

1. Matthew Crosby, Brad Simpson, James McVey, Connor Ball, Tristran Evans.

2. Marta, Ramona, Charmaine, Sheila, Diane.

3. Road to Ruen, Felt mountain, Life on other planets, I should coco, Diamond hoo ha.

4. Everything I own, Stand by me, Move closer, You win again, Star trekkin.

5. Dance again, Booty, Live it up, Waiting for tonight, On the floor.

6. How soon is now? Hit that perfect beat, Girlfriend in a coma, Shpolifters of the world unite, What difference does it make?

7. Bradley McIntosh, Terry Balsamo, Fred Durst, John Otto, Sam Rivers.

8. I don't want to be a soldier, Apple scruffs, How do you sleep? Gimme some truth, Crippled inside.

9. Too young to die, Cosmic girl, Canned heat, Kiss the girl, Space cowboy..

10. Shereen Cutkelvin, Lisa Origiasso, Asami Zdrenka, Amira McCarthg, Jessica Plummer.

11. Fundamental, Jollification, Four winds, Dizzy heights, Cloudcuckooland.

12. Like a prayer, Innuendo, Do the Bartman, Any dream will do, Black or white.

13. Yardbirds, Procol Harum, Cream, Derek and the Dominoes, Blind Faith.

14. Una Healy, Jade Ewen, Amelle Berrabah, Heidi Range, Mutya Buena.

15. Magic moments, I'm a believer, I just don't know what to do with myself, (They long to be) close to you, Anyone who had a heart.

16. Kandi Rain, Lloyd Daniels, Rikki Loney, Lucie Jones, Blonde Electra.

17. To the end, Parklife, End of a century, Country house, Girls and boys.

18. The day the rains came, As I love you, Memories are made of this, Dream lover, Here comes summer.

19. Up to date, New colours, Crossword puzzle, Shopping bag, Sound magazine, .

20. Coming up, A world without love, Come and get it, Step inside love, Imagine.

YOU'RE THE ONE No.3

ANSWERS

1. Matthew Crosby - is with The Common Linnets, the others are The Vamps.
2. Sheila - was a hit for Tommy Roe (and others), the rest were hits for The Bachelors.
3. Felt mountain - was a Goldfrapp album, the others were by Supergrass.
4. Move closer - was a 1985 chart topper, the others were at No.1 in 1987.
5. Waiting for tonight - all the other Jennifer Lopez singles were credited with Pitbull
6. Hit that perfect beat - was a hit for Bronski Beat, the others were Smiths singles.
7. Bradley McIntosh - is with S Club 7, the others are Limp Bizkit..
8. Apple scruffs - is a track from George Harrison's 'All things must pass', the others are from John Lennon's 'Imagine'.
9. Kiss the girl - was a hit for Peter Andre, the others were hits by Jamiroqui.
10. Lisa Origiasso is with The Veronicas, the others are Neon Jungle.
11. Fundamental - was a hit for Pet Shop Boys, the others were by The Lightning Seeds.
12. Like a prayer - was No.1 in 1989, the others topped the chart in 1991.
13. Procol Harum - Eric Clapton was never a member of that group, he was with all the others.
14. Una Healy - was with The Saturdays, the others were The Sugababes.
15. I'm a believer - was written by Neil Diamond, the others were by Burt Bacharach and Hal David.
16. Blonde Electra - featured in the 2014 X Factor, the others were finalists from 2009, who had a No.1 hit with 'you are not alone'.
17. Country house - is from 'The great escape' by Blur, the others are from 'Parklife'.
18. Memories are made of this - was a No.1 in 1956, the others topped the chart in 1959.
19. New colours - was an album by The New Seekers, the others were albums by The Partridge Family..
20. Imagine - was written by John Lennon, the others were by Paul McCartney.

ALPHABET No.2

The letters of the names of these recording artists have been arranged in alphabetical order. can you identify them?

1. LLMORSUY.
2. AEEHHILNOPRS.
3. AEIIMPRSTX.
4. AADILPU.
5. ABEEEGILPRRT.
6. AIIJLMMNY.
7. AHIJNNST.
8. BEEILNNORTY.
9. ACEGGIIIILLNOQTTU.
10. AEEHIIMNPTT.
11. ADEILMRTWY.
12. HIILLMSTW.
13. AHIJJMORST.
14. ACDEHIILLRRTT.
15. AEELORSY.
16. ABCEILLRRSUYY.
17. ACEIIIKLLMNORS.
18. ABBNORUY.
19. AAAEFGHIKNNRUV.
20. DDEEFIIKLLMO.

ALPHABET No.2

Answers

1. Olly Murs.
2. Helen Shapiro.
3. Maxi Priest.
4. Dua Lipa.
5. Peter Gabriel.
6. Jimmy Nail.
7. Saint Jhn.
8. Bonnie Tyler.
9. Gigiola Cinquetti.
10. Tinie Tempah.
11. Marty Wilde.
12. Will Smith.
13. Jorja Smith.
14. Little Richard.
15. Leo Sayer.
16. Billy Rae Cyrus.
17. Alison Limerick.
18. Burna Boy.
19. Frankie Vaughan.
20. Mike Oldfield.

THE NAME GAME No.9

By what names are the following better known:

1. Michael David Rosenburg.
2. Rosemary Brown.
3. Diane Catherine Sealy.
4. Everton Bonner.
5. Patrick Murray.
6. Natalie Renee McIntyre.
7. Avraham Reich Stadt.
8. Benjamin Paul Ballance-Drew.
9. Petrus Antonius Laurentius Kartner.
10. Domingo Samudio.
11. Robert Padslady.
12. Steven Demetre Georgiou.
13. Ashley Nicolette Franjepane.
14. Overton Amos Lemons.
15. Ian Fraser Kilminster.
16. DiFosco T Irvin Jnr.
17. Christopher Hamill.
18. Jeffery Lamar Williams.
19. Gary Anthony James Webb.
20. Sannie Charlotte Carlson.

THE NAME GAME No.9

Answers

1. Passenger.
2. Dana.
3. Dee C Lee.
4. Pliers.
5. Pato Banton.
6. Macy Gray.
7. Abi Ofarim.
8. Plan B.
9. Father Abraham.
10. Sam the Sham.
11. Rocky Sharpe.
12. Cat Stevens (AKA Yusuf Islam).
13. Halsey.
14. Smiley Lewis.
15. Lemmy.
16. Big Dee Irwin.
17. Limahl.
18. Young Thug.
19. Gary Numan.
20. Whigfield.

COMMON PEOPLE No.4

What do the following have in common?

1. Look wot you dun, Let's call it quits, Gudbuy T'Jane, Far far away, Take me bak 'ome.

2. Billy Corgan, Jimmy Chamberlin, Mike Byrne, Nicole Fiorentino, Jeff Schroeder.

3. Friday's child, 85% proof, Let it go, From now on, Keep on.

4. John Carter, Ken Lewis, Perry Ford, Neil Landon, Tony Burrows.

5. I feel free, White room, Strange brew, Badge, Anyone for tennis?

6. Anita Dobson, Paul Nicholas, Mike Reid, Michelle Gayle, Nick Berry.

7. Nick Carter, AJ McLean, Kevin Richardson, Howie Dorough, Brian Littrell.

8. Water for your soul, The soul sessions, The soul sessions volume II, Mind body and soul, Colour me free!

9. The Hollies, Dusty Springfield, The Swing Blue Jeans, Gene Pitney, Dave Clark Five.

10. Whatta man, Hold on, Give it up, turn it loose, Riddle, Whatever.

11. Siamese dream, Adore, Mellon Collie and the infinite sadness, Oceana, Monuments to an elegy.

12. Peter Tork, Duke Ellington, Marvin Gaye, Eva Cassidy, Van McCoy.

13. Spider Stacey, Cate O'Riordan, James Fearnley, Philip Chevron, Daryl Hunt.

14. Showaddywaddy, The Police, The Marcels, Connie Francis, Creedence Clearwater Revival.

15. All summer long, Sunflower, Smiley smile, That's why God made the radio, Wild honey.

16. Say you won't let go, Naked, Empty space, Recovery, Safe inside.

17. I kissed a girl, Everything is possible, Have you ever, Toxic, Can't get you out of my head.

18. 10cc, The Magic Lanterns, Godley and Creme, Hotlegs, The art of Noise.

19. Hat full of stars, Sisters of Avalon, She's so unusual, Bring ya to the brink, A night to remember.

20. Free, The Law, Bad Company, The Firm, Queen.

COMMON PEOPLE No.4

ANSWERS

1. They are all hit singles by Slade
2. They were all members of The Smashing Pumpkins.
3. They are all albums by Will Young.
4. They were all members of The Ivy League.
5. They are all hit singles by 'Cream'.
6. They have all had hit singles ... and were all in EastEnders.
7. They were all member of The Back Street Boys.
8. They are all albums by Joss Stone.
9. They all appeared on the first ever edition of Top of the Pops.
10. They were all hit singles for En Vogue.
11. They are all albums by The Smashing Pumpkins.
12. They were all born in Washington DC.
13. They were all members of The Pogues.
14. They all reached No.1 with songs about the moon - Under the moon of love, Walking on the moon, Blue moon, Carolina moon, Bad moon rising.
15. They are all albums by The Beach Boys.
16. They are all hit singles by James Arthur.
17. They all reached No.1 and were all co-written by Cathy Dennis.
18. Lol Creme was a member of each group.
19. They are all albums by Cyndi Lauper.
20. They have all featured Paul Rogers.

THE FIRST No.3

1. Whose first album was called 'Tuesday night music club'?
2. What was the title of Mariah Carey's first hit single?
3. Whose first No.1 album was called 'The raw and the cooked'?
4. Whose first hit single was 'Livin' on the front line'?
5. What was the first hit for the Tremeloes without Brian Poole?
6. Who was the first solo artiste to appear on BBC's 'Top of the pops'?
7. Whose first hit was 'Kiss this thing goodbye'?
8. 'The Hindu Times' is the opening track on which Oasis album?
9. 'Birds without wings' was the first single released by whom?
10. What was the first UK No.1 album by Elton John?
11. Whose first hit was 'Mandy'?
12. Mirror Man was the first single released by which 80's group?
13. What is the first track on Pink Floyd's 'The Wall'?
14. Whose first hit was 'The mother we share'?
15. What was the title of Malcolm McLaren's first hit single?
16. 'Shout' was the first track on which Tears for Fears album?
17. Fallin' was the first hit for which American singer?
18. Who was the first 'Spice Girl' to leave the group?
19. What was the debut album by the Cardigans called?
20. What is the first track on Paul Simon's album 'Graceland'?

THE FIRST No.3

Answers

1. Sheryl Crow.

2. Vision of love.

3. Fine Young Cannibals.

4. Eddy Grant.

5. Here comes my baby.

6. Dusty Springfield (in Episode 1 in 1964).

7. Del Amitri.

8. Heathen chemistry.

9. David Gray.

10. Don't shoot me I'm only the piano player.

11. Barry Manilow (although the original was by Scott English and was called 'Brandy').

12. Talk Talk.

13. In the flesh?

14. The Chvrches.

15. Buffalo Gals.

16. Songs from the big chair.

17. Alicia Keys.

18. Geri Halliwell - in 1998.

19. Emmerdale.

20. The boy in the bubble.

BLANK SPACE No.10

Fill in the blanks to reveal bands that have had chart hits:

1. E _ S _ B _ A _ S
2. B _ M _   T _ E   _ A _ S
3. R _ G _   A _ A _ N _ T   _ H _   M _ C _ I _ E
4. T _ M _ E _ A _ C _   S _ V _ N
5. M _ G _ E _ I _   M _ N
6. Y _ A _ S   _ N _   Y _ A _ S
7. M _ M _ O _ D   _ N _   S _ N _
8. Y _ U _ G   _ A _ C _ L _
9. T _ N   _ E _ R _   A _ T _ R
10. M _ J _ R   _ A _ E _
11. L _ E _ T _ N _ N _   P _ G _ O _
12. J _ D _ A _ D
13. G _ E _ N   _ E _ L _
14. C _ E _ I _   T _   T _ E   _ A _ I _ N
15. F _ E _ E _
16. L _ G _ T _ O _ S _   F _ M _ L _
17. S _ V _ G _   G _ R _ E _
18. R _ S _   R _ Y _ E
19. C _ U _ B _ W _ M _ A
20. T _ R _ E   _ O _   N _ G _ T

BLANK SPACE No.10

ANSWERS

1. Easybeats.
2. Bomb the Bass.
3. Rage against the Machine.
4. Temperance Seven.
5. Magnetic Man.
6. Years and Years.
7. Mumford and Sons.
8. Young Rascals.
9. Ten Years After.
10. Major Lazer.
11. Lieutenant Pigeon.
12. Jedward.
13. Green Jelly.
14. Credit to the Nation.
15. Freeez.
16. Lighthouse Family.
17. Savage Garden.
18. Rose Royce.
19. Chumbawamba.
20. Three Dog Night.

MIX IT UP No.6

Can you unravel the anagrams to identify these hit making bands?

1. LOANED COAL BOY
2. PINK TOSS
3. ZONAL BOOBY
4. HA HA WE MISS UFO SIDE
5. NO DUO IN FAST
6. STEAM VILE BED
7. CLAIMS PER ARM
8. FULL TOY BOA
9. NEVER DREAD PESTO MELT
10. BORES BROTH SIGN
11. TUT BRUCE LEA
12. GAGS CANE FINCH
13. APES HIT ROAD
14. BODMIN NOON BRATS
15. MAKE REPS SPIN
16. HANDY CURE
17. REST STOP IN RISE
18. GET LINER HUB VERY TIGHT
19. TOUCHY IONS
20. CRYING BOUT

MIX IT UP No.6

Answers

1. YOLANDA BE COOL
2. INK SPOTS
3. BABYLON ZOO
4. SWEDISH HOUSE MAFIA
5. FOUNDATIONS
6. BAD MEETS EVIL
7. PRIMAL SCREAM
8. FALL OUT BOY
9. ARRESTED DEVELOPMENT
10. GIBSON BROTHERS
11. CULTURE BEAT
12. CHANGING FACES
13. PORTISHEAD
14. TOM ROBINSON BAND
15. SNEAKER PIMPS
16. HUE AND CRY
17. POINTER SISTERS
18. EVERYTHING BUT THE GIRL
19. SONIC YOUTH
20. BIG COUNTRY

WHO ARE YOU? No.10

Which name is missing from these song titles?

1   ____ _____ (Slim Whitman)
2   ____ in disguise (with glasses) (John Fred)
3   My name is ____ (Manfred Mann)
4   ___ (Olivia Newton John)
5   C'mon _____ (PJ Harvey)
6   _____ do ya love me (White Plains)
7   ___ (Michael Jackson)
8   Mustang _____ (Wilson Pickett)
9   _____ (Scott Walker)
10 Wait for me ____-____ (Marmalade)
11 The diary of _____ Wimp (Electric Light Orchestra)
12 _____ the elephant (Toy Dolls)
13 Doctor _____ (The Beatles)
14 You can call me __ (Paul Simon)
15 Rockin' _____ (Michael Jackson)
16 Poppa ___ (The Sweet)
17 Oh _____ (Shaggy)
18 _____ May (Rod Stewart)
19 My brother ____ (Free)
20 A message to _____ (Kentucky bluebird) (Adam Faith)

WHO ARE YOU? No.10

Answers

1	Rose Marie.

2	Judy.

3	Jack.

4	Sam.

5	Billy.

6	Julie.

7	Ben.

8	Sally.

9	Joanna ..... or Jackie.

10	Mary-Anne.

11	Horace.

12	Nellie.

13	Robert.

14	Al.

15	Robin.

16	Joe.

17	Carolina.

18	Maggie.

19	Jake.

20	Martha.

WORDS No.10

Can you identify these famous songs from their opening lyrics:

1. The marching band came down along Main Street. The soldier-blues fell in behind ....

2. I got my first real six string, bought it at the five and dime ....

3. We've come a long, long way together, through the hard times and the good ....

4. You say 'I love you boy', but I know you lie. I trust you all the same ....

5. You are all the woman I need, and baby you know it. You can make this beggar ....

6. Gold Coast slave ship bound for cotton field. Sold in the market ...

7. I want my MTV. Now, look at them yo-yo's, that's the way you do it .....

8. Baby, can't you see I'm calling? A guy like you should wear a warning .....

9. You never close your eyes anymore when I kiss your lips. And there's no tenderness like before in your fingertips ....

10. What about sunrise? What about rain? What about all the things you said ....

11. Now here's a little story. To tell it is a must. About an unsung hero ....

12. I'm feeling sexy and free, like glitter's falling on me. You're like a shot ....

13. Stuck inside these four walls. Sent inside forever. Never seeing no one nice again .....

14. If I should stay, I would only be in your way. So I'll go, but I know I'll think of you ....

15. Dark in the city, night is a wire. Steam in the subway, earth is afire ...

16. This is a number one champion sound. Yeah, Estelle, we about to get down ....

17. Goodbye to you, my trusted friend. We've known each other since .....

18. Desert loving in your eyes. If I listen to your lies would you say ....

19. I see trees of green, red roses too. I see them bloom for me and you ....

20. I wanna know whoever told you I was letting go of the only joy that I have ever known ....

WORDS No.10

Answers

1. Billy, don't be a hero (Paper Lace).
2. Summer of 69 (Bryan Adams).
3. Praise you (Fat Boy Slim).
4. Many of horror (Biffy Clyro) ... or ...When we collide (Matt Cardle).
5. Bend me, shape me (Amen Corner).
6. Brown sugar (Rolling Stones).
7. Money for nothing (Dire Straits).
8. Toxic (Britney Spears).
9. You've lost that lovin' feelin' (Righteous Brothers).
10. Earth song (Michael Jackson).
11. My old man's a dustman (Lonnie Donegan).
12. Domino (Jessie J).
13. Band on the run (Wings).
14. I will always love you (Whitney Houston).
15. Hungry like the wolf (Duran Duran).
16. American boy (Estelle featuring Kanye West).
17. Seasons in the sun (Terry Jacks).
18. Karma chameleon (Culture Club).
19. What a wonderful world (Louis Armstrong).
20. Swear it again (Westlife).

ANY COLOUR YOU LIKE No.4

Which colour is missing from these song titles?

1. _____ flag (Dido)
2. _____ hat for a _____ day (Nik Heyward)
3. The _____ Manalishi (with the two prong crown) (Fleetwood Mac)
4. _____ blooded woman (Kylie Minogue)
5. _____ country woman (Led Zeppelin)
6. Maxwell's _____ hammer (The Beatles)
7. _____ champagne (Ariana Grande)
8. _____ crush (REM)
9. Ride a _____ swan (T Rex)
10. Shades of _____ (Mission)
11. Shades of _____ (The Monkees)
12. _____ (Fine Young Cannibals)
13. Strike me _____ (Deborah Harry)
14. _____ Christmas (Bing Crosby)
15. She wears _____ feathers (Guy Mitchell)
16. _____ cliffs of Dover (Acker Bilk)
17. Long John _____ (Jefferson Airplane)
18. _____ fields (Beverley Sisters)
19. _____ wine (Elkie Brooks)
20. African and _____ (China Crisis)

ANY COLOUR YOU LIKE No.4

Answers

1	White.
2	Blue, blue.
3	Green.
4	Red.
5	Black.
6	Silver.
7	Pink.
8	Orange.
9	White.
10	Green.
11	Gray.
12	Blue.
13	Pink.
14	White.
15	Red.
16	White.
17	Silver.
18	Green.
19	Lilac.
20	White.

EMPTY SPACES No.11

Fill in the blanks to reveal musicians who have had chart hits:

1. L _ N _ A   _ O _ S _ A _ T
2. F _ N _ E _   Q _ A _ E
3. T _ N _   M _ R _ E
4. B _ T _ Y   _ C _ E _ N
5. S _ E _ Y _   C _ O _
6. J _ N _ T _ A _   K _ N _
7. A _ A _ H _   I _ D _ A _
8. R _ G _ R   _ A _ T _ E _
9. J _ D _ E   _ Y _ H _
10. V _ N _ E   _ O _
11. S _ O _ T   _ A _ K _ R
12. J _ R _ I _   S _ A _ K _
13. D _ S _ Y   _ P _ I _ G _ I _ L _
14. J _ L _ E   _ R _ I _ E
15. F _ E _ A   _ A _ N _
16. S _ N _ A _   Q _ I _ N
17. W _ I _ E   _ O _ N
18. Y _ O _ N _   F _ I _
19. S _ M   _ P _ R _ O
20. L _ N _   Z _ V _ R _ N _

EMPTY SPACES No.11

ANSWERS

1. Linda Ronstadt.
2. Finley Quaye.
3. Tina Marie.
4. Bitty McLean.
5. Sheryl Crow.
6. Jonathan King.
7. Apache Indian.
8. Roger Daltrey.
9. Jodie Aysha.
10. Vance Joy.
11. Scott Walker.
12. Jordin Sparks.
13. Dusty Springfield.
14. Julee Cruise.
15. Freda Payne.
16. Sinead Quinn.
17. White Town.
18. Yvonne Fair.
19. Sam Sparro.
20. Lena Zavaroni.

THE NAME GAME No.10

By what names are the following better known:

1. David Spencer.
2. Joseph Montanez.
3. John Courville.
4. Thomasina Winifred Montgomery.
5. William Michael Griffin.
6. Kathleen O'Rourke.
7. Chancelor Jonathan Bennett.
8. Dora May Broadbent.
9. Charles Anthony Graci.
10. Cameron Jibril Thomaz.
11 Virginia Wynette Pugh.
12. Trevor Herbert Stanford.
13. Dwayne Michael Carter.
14. Agatha Nathalia Weston.
15. Ruth Lee Jones.
16. Bruce Fielder.
17. Lynda Susan Belcher.
18. Evelyn May Beatson.
19. Shaffer Chimere Smith.
20. Amethyst Amelia Kelly.

THE NAME GAME No.10

Answers

1. Ricky Valance

2. Monti Rock (aka Disco-Tex).

3. Johnny Preston (His middle name was Preston, but we didn't give you that!).

4. Tammi Terrell.

5. Rakim.

6. Kathy Kirby.

7. Chance the Rapper.

8. Dora Bryan.

9. Charlie Gracie.

10. Khalifa.

11. Tammy Wynette.

12. Russ Conway.

13. Lil Wayne.

14. Kim Weston.

15. Dinah Washington.

16. Sigla.

17. Lyn Paul.

18. Eve Graham.

19. Ne-Yo.

20. Iggy Azalia.

THERE'S A PLACE No.6

Which place name is missing from these song titles?

1 _____ song (Waterboys)
2 The road to _____ (Robbie Williams)
3 Last night in ____ (Dave Dee, Dozy, Beaky, Mick and Tich)
4 A message to Martha (_____ bluebird) (Adam Faith)
5 Roses of _____ (Vince Hill)
6 _____ (Petula Clark)
7 Fairytale of ___ ____ (The Pogues with Kirsty MacColl)
8 _____ (Bruce Springsteen)
9 Loco in _____ (Four Tops)
10 _____ (Middle of the Road)
11 Lights of _____ (Scott Walker)
12 _____ (Typically Tropical)
13 We're going to _____ ! (Vengaboys)
14 _____ (Kim Wilde)
15 _____ sea (Ed Sheeran)
16 _____ boys (Sham 69)
17 _____ man (The Move)
18 Going down to _____ (Bangles)
19 _____ (Toto)
20 _____ lace (Big Bopper)

THERE'S A PLACE No.6

Answers

1	Glastonbury.

2	Mandalay.

3	Soho.

4	Kentucky.

5	Picardy.

6	Majorca.

7	New York.

8	Nebraska.

9	Acapulco.

10	Sacramento.

11	Cincinnati.

12	Barbabos.

13	Ibiza (it was a re-working of the above song).

14	Cambodia.

15	Tenerife.

16	Hersham.

17	California.

18	Liverpool.

19	Africa.

20	Chantilly.

LUCKY NUMBER No.6

Which cardinal or ordinal numbers are missing from these song titles?

1   _____ minute man (Missy 'Misdemeanor' Elliott)
2   _____ seconds (Neneh Cherry)
3   Johnny _____ (Bruce Springsteen)
4   _____ degrees (Kylie and Dannii Minogue)
5   Back at _____ (Lulu with Westlife)
6   _____ _____ (Matt Cardle)
7   _____ , _____ , _____ , _____ , _____ , _____ , _____ (Bucks Fizz)
8   Cloud _____ (George Harrison)
9   _____ time loser (Rod Stewart)
10 Twixt _____ and _____ (Pat Boone)
11 _____ for the price of _____ (Abba)
12 _____ , _____ , _____ , _____ (Plain White T's)
13 Song _____ (Blur)
14 _____ Subaru (Fountains of Wayne)
15 _____ days (Mary J Blige)
16 _____ ring circus (Barry Biggs)
17 Brokan heart (_____ valleys) (Big Country)
18 _____ . _____ . _____ . _____ . Get with the wicked (Richard Blackwood)
19 In the year _____ _____ (Exordium and terminus) (Zager and Evans)
20 Take _____ (Dave Brubeck)

LUCKY NUMBER No.6

Answers

1	One.
2	Seven.
3	Ninety nine.
4	One hundred.
5	One.
6	Ten, ten.
7	Ten, nine, eight, seven, six, five, four.
8	Nine.
9	Three.
10	Twelve, twenty.
11	Two, one.
12	One, two, three, four.
13	Two.
14	Ninety two.
15	Seven.
16	Three.
17	Thirteen.
18	One. Two. Three. Four.
19	Twenty five, twenty five.
20	Five.

TWO OF US No.4

Can you complete the names of these duos?

1. Dale and ?
2. Ali and ?
3. Sly and ?
4. Denise and ?
5. David and ?
6. Bini and ?
7. Tillmann and ?
8. Yin and ?
9. Pearl Carr and ?
10. Banx and?
11. Frank and ?
12. Andy and David ?
13. Marvin and ?
14. Nino Tempo and ?
15. Pinky and ?
16. White and ?
17. Reva Rice and ?
18. Skipworth and ?
19. Ed Rush and ?
20. Miki and ?

TWO OF US No.4

Answers

1. Grace.
2. Frazier.
3. Robbie.
4. Johnny (Van Outen and Vaughan).
5. Jonathan.
6. Martini.
7. Reis.
8. Yan.
9. Teddy Johnson.
10. Ranx.
11. Walters.
12. Williams.
13. Tamora.
14. April Stevens.
15. Perky.
16. Torch.
17. Greg Ellis.
18. Turner.
19. Optical.
20. Griff.

WE ARE FAMILY No.3

Which human relations are missing from these song titles?

1   Super _ _ _ _ (Billy Connolly)

2   _ _ _ _ weer all crazee now (Slade)

3   Yes my darling _ _ _ _ _ _ _ _ (Eydie Gorme)

4   _ _ _ _ loves mambo (Perry Como)

5   _ _ _ _ Lisa (Mastodon)

6   Dance like yo _ _ _ _ _ (Meghan Trainor)

7   _ _ _ _ _ _ _ _ in arms (Dire Straits)

8   _ _ _ _ _ _ _ _ of darkness (Tom Jones)

9   _ _ _ _ oom mow mow (Gary Glitter)

10   Beat _ _ _ _ _ _ _ (Cast)

11   _ _ _ _ _ Jonny (The Killers)

12   Me and Bobby and Bobby's _ _ _ _ _ _ _ (Abba)

13   _ _ _ _ _ _ _ _ and _ _ _ _ _ (Neil Diamond)

14   Don't cry _ _ _ _ _ (Elvis Presley)

15   _ _ _ _ - who dat man? (Richard Blackwood)

16   _ _ _ _ _ _ _ _ (Pearl Jam)

17   _ _ _ _ _ _ figure (George Michael)

18   _ _ _ _ _ _ (Bros)

19   My _ _ _ my _ _ _ (Vera Lynn)

20   Poor man's _ _ _ (Rockin' Berries).

WE ARE FAMILY No.3

Answers

1	Gran.
2	Mama.
3	Daughter.
4	Papa.
5	Aunt.
6	Daddy.
7	Brothers.
8	Daughter.
9	Papa.
10	Mama.
11	Uncle.
12	Brother.
13	Husbands, wives.
14	Daddy.
15	Mama.
16	Daughter.
17	Father.
18	Sister.
19	Son.
20	Son.

BLANK SPACE No.11

Fill in the blanks to reveal bands that have had chart hits:

1. D _ A _ O _   A _ I _ E
2. E _ E _ N _ L
3. L _ V _   S _ U _ P _ U _ E
4. S _ A _ H _ N _   P _ M _ K _ N _
5. R _ Z _ L _ O _
6. S _ E _ E _   D _ V _ S   _ R _ U _
7. N _ C _ E _ B _ C _
8. A _ C _ D _ A
9. N _ W   _ E _ K _ R _
10. R _ Y _ O _ D _   G _ R _ S
11. W _ L _   T _   P _ W _ R
12. G _ L _ F _ A _ P
13. L _ S _   S _ A _ O _   P _ P _ E _ S
14. I _ L _   A _ D   _ A _ T _ Y
15. M _ L _ I   _ A _ I _ L _
16. P _ A _ T _ C   _ E _ N _
17. B _ A _ D   _ E _   H _ A _ I _ S
18. N _ O _   J _ N _ L _
19. B _ C _ S _ R _ E _   B _ Y _
20. O _ E   _ R _ E   _ O _ C _

BLANK SPACE No.11

ANSWERS

1. Dead or Alive.
2. Eternal.
3. Love Sculpture.
4. Smashing Pumpkins.
5. Rezillos.
6. Spencer Davis Group.
7. Nickelback.
8. Arcadia.
9. New Seekers.
10. Reynolds Girls.
11. Will to Power.
12. Goldfrapp.
13. Last Shadow Puppets.
14. Iglu and Hartly.
15. Milli Vanilli.
16. Plastic Penny.
17. Brand New Heavies.
18. Neon Jungle.
19. Backstreet Boys.
20. One True Voice.

ALL SHOOK UP No.6

Can you unravel the anagrams to identify these music personalities?

1. RING SEED MELON
2. RIB ALAN HYND
3. FED ANY PEAR
4. RAN IN KEY BEND
5. SO LAZE LIP
6. THE SLY TEEN GAP
7. HEARS A WAR MOTH
8. JAR RISETH
9. SLY LETTER RAGE
10. SHES NO SARDINE NUN
11. A HAY MURDER
12. MADDY ON A CLAM
13. BE XMAS GRAVY
14. I TAKE A BARN
15. CASE TO SLY MOON
16. CLOSE TRAY
17. FEED ANY PEAR
18. A CHILE BUMBLE
19. MARK CAKE WIN
20. A BAD ARSON BRICK

ALL SHOOK UP No.6

Answers

1. GLENN MEDEIROS
2. BRIAN HYLAND
3. FREDA PAYNE
4. BRIAN KENNEDY
5. LISA LOPEZ
6. STEPHEN GATELY
7. SARAH WHATMORE
8. JET HARRIS
9. LESLEY GARRETT
10. SUNSHINE ANDERSON
11. MURRAY HEAD
12. AMY MACDONALD
13. MAX BYGRAVES
14. ANITA BAKER
15. STACEY SOLOMON
16. ROY CASTLE
17. FREDA PAYNE
18. MICHAEL BUBLE
19. RICK WAKEMAN
20. BARBARA DICKSON

WORDS No.11

Can you identify these famous songs from their opening lyrics:

1. I never thought I'd see the day when you became what you've become ....

2. Dirty old river, must you keep rolling, flowing into the night ....

3. I heard that you're settled down, that you found a girl andyou're married now ....

4. All night long you've been looking at me. You know you're the dance hall cutie ....

5. I knew you'd go far in my white convertible car. Recline in my seat ....

6. Don't need nobody just me and you. Like the way you walk, like the things you do ...

7. I've crossed the deserts for miles, swam water for time, searching places .....

8. Oh, my love, my darling. I've hungered for your touch a long, lonely time .....

9. Oh, the heads that turn make my back burn. And the heads that turn make my back ....

10. I don't care what songs you sing, or how you think of all those pointless things ....

11. A well'a bless ma soul, what'sa wrong with me? I'm itchin' like a man in a fuzzy tree. My friends say I'm actin' wild as a bug ...

12. On your mark, ready, set, let's go. Dance floor pro, I know you know ....

13. I heard you on the wireless back in fifty two, lying awake intent on tuning in .....

14. Well, you must be a girl with shoes like that. She said "You know me well" ....

15. Come puede ser verdad. Last night I dreamt of san Pedro. Just like I'd never gone ...

16. I was born long ago. I am the chosen, I am the one. I have come to save the day ....

17. Your baby doesn't love you anymore. Golden days before they end .....

18. All I need is a TV show. That and the radio. Down on my luck again ....

19. Homegrown alligator, see you later, gotta hit the road, gotta hit the road ....

20. I would take the stars out of the sky for you. Stop the rain from falling ....

WORDS No.11

Answers

1. This garden (Levellers).
2. Waterloo sunset (The Kinks).
3. Someone like you (Adele).
4. Tiger feet (Mud).
5. TV (Flying Lizards).
6. One and one is one (Medicine Head).
7. Pure shores (All Saints).
8. Unchained melody (Righteous Brothers).
9. She sells sanctuary (Cult).
10. Sugar coated iceberg (Lightning Seeds).
11. All shook up (Elvis Presley).
12. Gettin' jiggy wit it (Will Smith).
13. Video killed the radio star (Buggles).
14. Chelsea dagger (The Fratellis).
15. La isla bonita (Madonna).
16. Are you gonna go my way? (Lenny Kravitz).
17. It's over (Roy Orbison).
18. Turn it on again (Genesis).
19. Shotgun (George Ezra).
20. You to me are everything (Real Thing).

WHO ARE YOU? No.11

Which name is missing from these song titles?

1   _ _ _ _ _   Mulligan   (Ed Sheeran)

2   Aunt   _ _ _ _   (Mastodon)

3   _ _ _ _   teen   (Cockney Rebel)

4   The killing of   _ _ _ _ _ _ _   (Rod Stewart)

5   _ _ _ _ _ _   Reggae   (The Piglets)

6   My   _ _ _ _   (Bay City Rollers)

7   _ _ _   Lind (the only way is down)   (Pulp)

8   _ _ _ _ _   Bond theme   (Moby)

9   Uncle   _ _ _ _ _ _   (Paul and Linda McCartney)

10   _ _ _ _ _ _   's walk   (Led Zeppelin)

11   Tell   _ _ _ _ _   I love her   (Ricky Valance)

12   _ _ _ _ _ _   's army   (Elvis Costello)

13   _ _ _ _ _ _   's farm   (Bob Dylan)

14   When   _ _ _ _ _   comes back to the farm   (The Move)

15   _ _ _ _ _ _   's farm   (Wings)

16   _ _ _ _ _ _ _   (Toto)

17   Pool hall   _ _ _ _ _ _ _   (The Faces)

18   _ _ _ _ _ _ _   (Alan Price and Georgie Fame)

19   _ _ _ _ _   (the fastest milkman in the west)   (Benny Hill)

20   Right said   _ _ _ _   (Bernard Cribbens)

WHO ARE YOU? No.11

Answers

1	Nancy.
2	Lisa.
3	Judy.
4	Georgie.
5	Johnny.
6	Lisa.
7	Bob.
8	James.
9	Albert.
10	Walter.
11	Laura.
12	Oliver.
13	Maggie.
14	Alice.
15	Junior.
16	Rosanna.
17	Richard.
18	Rosetta.
19	Ernie.
20	Fred.

THE NAME GAME No.11

By what names are the following better known:

1. Angus Murdo McKenzie.
2. Cornell Iral Haynes.
3. Keidran Jones.
4. Martin David Robinson.
5. Timothy Zachary Mosley.
6. Brenda Mae Tarpley.
7. Richard Kylea Cowie.
8. Donald McKinley Glover.
9. Philip Wallach Blondheim.
10. Guy James Robin.
11. Revoyda Frierson.
12. Gazzy Garcia.
13. Mary Sandeman.
14. Felix De Laet.
15. Willie Maxwell.
16. Leslie Wunderman.
17. Ernest Jennings Ford.
18. Robin Miriam Carlsson.
19. Kelly Biggs.
20. Anthony Moses Davis.

THE NAME GAME No.11

Answers

1. Karl Denver.
2. Nelly.
3. Iyaz.
4. Marty Robbins.
5. Timbaland.
6. Brenda Lee.
7. Wiley Kat (or just Wiley).
8. Childish Gambino.
9. Scott McKenzie.
10. Jonas Blue.
11. Ketty Lester.
12. Lil Pump.
13. Aneka.
14. Lost Frequencies.
15. Fetty Wap.
16. Taylor Dayne.
17. Tennessee Ernie Ford.
18. Robyn.
19. Kele Le Roc.
20. Beanie Man.

EMPTY SPACES No.12

Fill in the blanks to reveal musicians who have had chart hits:

1. K _ M _ E _ L _ Y   _ A _ S _
2. C _ R _ I _   S _ I _ E _ S
3. M _ R _ D _ T _   B _ O _ K _
4. B _ B _ Y   _ A _ I _
5. N _ C _ L _   S _ H _ R _ I _ G _ R
6. B _ L _ I _   M _ R _ S
7. K _ Y   _ T _ R _
8. C _ Y _ T _ L   W _ T _ R _
9. J _ H _ N _   L _ G _ N
10. F _ A _ K _ E   _ A _ G _ A _
11. V _ C _ Y   _ E _ N _ R _ S
12. B _ O _ K   _ E _ T _ N
13. D _ V _ D   _ H _ I _ T _ E
14. M _ R _   O _ E _
15. R _ N _ Y   _ R _ W _ O _ D
16. G _ O _ G _   M _ C _ A _
17. D _ N _ S _   L _ S _ L _ E
18. J _ N _   M _ D _ N _ L _
19. S _ A _   M _ L _ I _ S
20. A _ R _ A _   G _ R _ I _ Z

EMPTY SPACES No.12

ANSWERS

1. Kimberley Walsh.
2. Curtis Stigers.
3. Meredith Brooks.
4. Bobby Darin.
5. Nicole Scherzinger.
6. Billie Myres.
7. Kay Starr.
8. Crystal Waters.
9. Johnny Logan.
10. Frankie Vaughan.
11. Vicky Leandros.
12. Brook Benton.
13. David Christie.
14. Mark Owen.
15. Randy Crawford.
16. George McCrae.
17. Denise LaSalle.
18. Jane McDonald.
19. Shawn Mullins.
20. Adrian Gurvitz.

WOULD I LIE TO YOU? No.5

Are the following statements true or false?

1. Jane McDonald's first TV appearance was as a dancer on Black Lace's 'Superman'.
2. Stephen Tompkinson was the voice of Bob the Builder.
3. Bruce Woodley was a founder member of both The Seekers and The New Seekers.
4. Polly Filla was the lead singer with X Ray Spex.
5. The Blockheads and Dr Feelgood guitarist, Wilko Johnson, appeared in 'Game of Thrones' as Ser llyn Payne.
6. The Bluebells' 1993 No.1 hit 'Young at heart' was first released in 1983 when it reached No.2 in the charts.
7. Richard Ashcroft was lead singer with The Verve.
8. The band, Level 42, originates from the Isle of Wight..
9. Bass guitarist, John Lantree, and drummer, Honey Lantree, of The Honeycombs were husband and wife.
10. Rick Allen, drummer with Def Leppard, has only one arm.
11. Ed Sheeran appeared as himself in the film 'Bridget Jones's Diary'.
12. Journey South comprises of brothers Charlie and Craig Reid.
13. The Vengaboys 1999 No.1 'We're going to Ibiza' was a re-working of Typically Tropical's 1975 No.1 'Barbados'.
14. Both the Beatles and The Rolling Stones had more No.1 singles in the UK than they did in the USA.
15. 'Gin soaked woman' and 'The frog Queen' were hit singles for The Devine Comedy.
16. Luther Vandross was once a backing singer in Nile Rodgers' group 'Chic'.
17. Danish singer, Sannie Charlotte Carlson is professionally known as either Sannie, Naan or Whigfield.
18. Hilary Duff achieved five UK Top Ten hits between 2003 -2015.
19. Emeli Sande's first name is Adele.
20. Aliasghar Movasat is professionally known as DJ Crocodile.

WOULD I LIE TO YOU? No.5

Answers

1. True.

2. False - it was Neil Morrisey.

3. False - he was a founder of The Seekers, but it was Keith Potger who founded both.

4. False - it was Polly Styrene .

5. True.

6. False - it was first released in 1984 when it peaked at No.8..

7. True.

8. True - Mark King and the Gould brothers all came from there.

9. False - they were brother and sister.

10. True - he lost it in a motor accident in 1984.

11. False - it was in 'Bridget Jones's Baby' that he appeared.

12. False - it's Andy and Carl Pemberton. The Reid's are The Proclaimers.

13. True.

14. False - The Beatles had 17 UK and 21 US, The Stones had 8 in each.

15. False - it was 'Gin soaked boy' and 'The frog Princess'.

16. True.

17. True.

18. False -she only had two.

19. True.

20. False - he is DJ Aligator.

HAPPY BIRTHDAY No.6

Can you identify these musicians?

1. Singer born in Coventry, England on 30 November 1937.

2. Singer born in New York, USA on 25 June 1945.

3. Drummer born in London, England on 23 August 1946.

4. Singer born in Nantucket, USA on 22 December 1993.

5. DJ and singer born in Londonderry, Northern Ireland on 11 February 1967.

6. Singer born in Liverpool, England on 9 October 1940.

7. Singer born in Bishopbriggs, Scotland on 25 August 1987.

8 Singer born in Modena, Italy on 12 October 1935.

9. Drummer and actor born in Los Angeles, USA on 8 March 1945.

10 Singer born in Deptford, England on 27 February 1951.

11 Singer born in Skewen, Wales on 8 June 1951.

12. Singer born in Hereford, England on 30 December 1986.

13. Bassist and singer born in Bishopbriggs, Scotland on 14 May 1943.

14. Singer born in Hertford, England on 7 June 1993.

15. Singer and guitarist born in Macclesfield, England on 29 November 1933.

16. Bassist born in Kirkcaldy, Scotland on 12 April 1978.

17. Rapper born in Toronto, Canada on 24 October 1986.

18 Singer born in Dover, England on 11 April 1987.

19. Guitarist born in Weston Super Mare, England on 14 April 1945.

20. Singer born in Solna, Sweden on 16 December 1997.

HAPPY BIRTHDAY No.6

Answers

1. Frank Ifield.
2. Carly Simon.
3. Keith Moon.
4. Meghan Trainor.
5. Paul McLoone.
6. John Lennon.
7. Amy Macdonald.
8. Luciano Pavarotti.
9. Micky Dolenz.
10. Steve Harley.
11. Bonnie Tyler.
12. Ellie Goulding.
13. Jack Bruce.
14. George Ezra.
15. John Mayall.
16. Guy Berryman.
17. Drake.
18. Joss Stone.
19. Ritchie Blackmore.
20. Zara Larsson.

JOIN TOGETHER No.5

These groups were known for backing which musician?

1. The Cresters.
2. The Band of Thieves.
3. His City Gents.
4. The Playboys.
5. His Dominoes.
6. The New Bohemians.
7. The Fentones.
8. The Fenmen.
9. The Detroit Wheels.
10. The FBI.
11. The Mechanics.
12. Company.
13. The Criminal Element.
14. His Quartet.
15. The Rumour.
16. The Rudies.
17. The Blue Jeans.
18. The Four Seasons.
19. The Zodiacs.
20. The Rude Boy of House.

JOIN TOGETHER No.5

Answers

1. Mike Sagar.
2. Luke Goss.
3. Dick Charlesworth.
4. Gary Lewis.
5. Billy Ward.
6. Eddie Brickell.
7. Shane Fenton (later to be Alvin Stardust).
8. Bern Elliott.
9. Mitch Ryder.
10. Redhead Kingpin.
11. Mike (Rutherford).
12. Julia (Nixon).
13. Wally Jump Junior.
14. Mario Marini.
15. Graham Parker.
16. Freddie Notes.
17. Bob B Sox.
18. Frankie Valli.
19. Maurice Williams.
20. Housemaster Boyz.

YOU'RE THE ONE No. 4

Can you spot the odd one out in each case?

1. Lyn Dobson, Karl Jenkins, Robert Wyatt, Michelle Phillips, Kevin Ayres.

2. The great pretender, When I fall in love, Twilight time, Smoke gets in your eyes, My prayer.

3. Charlotte Church, Rory Gallagher, Una Healy, Bob Geldoff, Andrea Corr.

4. Plastic letters, No exit, Loose screw, Pollinator, Panic of girls.

5. Someone you loved, Havana, New rules, Too good at goodbyes, Rockstar.

6. This is me, Rewrite the stars, More than a woman, A million dreams, From now on.

7. Love how it hurts, It's not about you, Famous, She's so lovely, A sky full of stars.

8. Pop life, Nothing but the beat, Listen, One love, Catch 22.

9. Garth Crooks, Kevin Reeves, Steve Archibald, Chris Hughton, Graham Roberts..

10. Coward of the county, Three times a lady, Rat trap, Take a chance on me, Uptown top ranking.

11. I got the blues, Sister Morphine, Wild horses, Dead flowers, Sympathy for the devil.

12. Denny Laine, , Jamelia, Jeff Lynne, Toyah, Ian Paice.

13. Satisfy you, Fill me in, Hidden agenda, Woman trouble, Rendezvous.

14. Sara Dallin, Jacquie O'Sullivan, Marcella Detroit, Siobhan Fahey, Keren Woodward.

15. Steve Howe, Joe English, Denny Siewell, Geoff Britton, Steve Holley.

16. Just a little bit better, This golden ring, Silhouettes, Show me girl, This door swings both ways, .

17. Tommy DeVito, Don Ciccone, Henry Vestine, Jerry Corbetta, Bob Gaudio.

18. All that she wants, Boom! Shake the room, Relight my fire, Living on my own, The one and only.

19. Little creatures, Remain in light, True stories, Born into this, Fear of music.

20 Eric Faulkner, Don Powell, Graham Coxon, George Harrison, Billy Duffy.

YOU'RE THE ONE No 4

ANSWERS

1. Michelle Phillips - was with The Mamas and Papas, the others were Soft Machine.

2. When I fall in love - was a hit for Nat King Cole (and others), the rest were by The Platters (and others!).

3. Charlotte Church - is Welsh, the others are Irish.

4. Loose screw - is an album by The Pretenders, the others are Blondie albums.

5. Someone you loved - was No.1 in 2019, the others topped the chart in 2017.

6. More than a woman - is from 'Saturday night fever', the others are from The greatest showman'.

7. A sky full of stars - was a hit single by Coldplay, the others were hits for Scouting For Girls.

8. Catch 22 - is an album by Tinchy Stryder, the others are David Guetta albums.

9. Kevin Reeves - played for Manchester City v Spurs in the 1981 FA Cup final. The others were in the Spurs squad who recorded 'Ossie's Dream' with Chas & Dave.

10. Coward of the county - was No.1 in 1980, the others topped the chart in 1978.

11. Sympathy for the devil - was from The Rolling Stones 'Beggar's Banquet', the others are from The Stones 'Sticky fingers'.

12. Ian Paice - was born in Nottingham, the others were born in Birmingham.

13. Satisfy you - was a hit single for Puff Daddy, the others were by Craig David.

14. Marcella Detroit - was with Shakespeare's Sister, the others were Bananarama (although Siobhan Fahey was in both).

15. Steve Howe - was a guitarist with 'Yes', the others were drummers with 'Wings'.

16. This golden ring - was a hit for The Fortunes, the others were by Herman's Hermits .

17. Henry Vestine - was with Canned Heat, the others were The Four Seasons.

18. The one and only - was a No.1 in 1991, the others topped the chart in 1993.

19. Born into this - is an album by The Cult, the others are Talking Heads albums.

20. Don Powell - was a drummer (with Slade) the others were guitarists.

BLANK SPACE No.12

Fill in the blanks to reveal bands that have had chart hits:

1. B _ A _ I _ ' S _ U _ D
2. P _ P _ Y _ A _ I _ Y
3. T _ P _ O _ D _ R
4. A _ O _ I _ R _ O _ T _ R
5. U _ T _ M _ T _ K _ O _
6. C _ I _ A _ B _ U _ S _ A _ D
7. F _ R _ T _ H _ I _ E
8. M _ X _ M _ P _ R _
9. L _ Q _ I _ G _ L _
10. R _ Z _ L _ K _ C _ S
11. S _ G _ R _ I _ L _ A _ G
12. T _ E _ M _ G _ T _ E G _ A _ T _
13. S _ L _ D _ E _ E _ S _ B _ U _ D _
14. D _ R _ Y _ O _ E _
15. S _ E _ T _ E _ S _ T _ O _
16. U _ L _ K _ D _ O _
17. B _ L _ I _ I
18. D _ E _ M _ E _ V _ R _
19. S _ E _ K _ R _ I _ P _
20. S _ N _ C _ O _ T _

BLANK SPACE No.12

ANSWERS

1. Blazin' Squad.
2. Poppy Family.
3. Toploader.
4. Atomic Rooster.
5. Ultimate Kaos.
6. Climax Blues Band.
7. First Choice.
8. Maximo Park.
9. Liquid Gold.
10. Rizzle Kicks.
11. Sugarhill Gang.
12. They Might Be Giants.
13. Splodgenessabounds.
14. Dirty Money.
15. Sweet Sensation.
16. Ugly Kid Joe.
17. Bellini.
18. Dream Weavers.
19. Sneaker Pimps.
20. Sonic Youth.

LIVIN' THING No.5

Which creatures are missing from these song titles?

1   Little red _ _ _ _ _ _ (Frank Chacksfield)

2   _ _ _ _ _ _ of love (Kate Bush)

3   Rock _ _ _ _ _ _ _ (B52's)

4   _ _ _ _ _ _ _ stance (Neneh Cherry)

5   Afternoon of the _ _ _ _ _ (Mike Post)

6   Stool _ _ _ _ _ _ (Kid Creole)

7   _ _ _ _ _ _ (Selena Gomez with Marshmello)

8   The _ _ _ _ _ and the _ _ _ _ (Alma Cogan)

9   Walk like a _ _ _ _ _ _ _ '98 (Tony Christie)

10   _ _ _ among the _ _ _ _ _ _ _ (Bros)

11   _ _ _ _ _ _ gone to heaven (Pixies)

12   When the _ _ _ _ _ _ broke free (Pink Floyd)

13   _ _ _ _ _ _ _ _ stone (Stone Roses)

14   Night _ _ _ (Gerry Rafferty)

15   _ _ _ _ _ _ _ _ _ (The Beatles)

16   Elusive _ _ _ _ _ _ _ _ _ (Val Doonican)

17   _ _ _ _ _ _ _ _ _ (Owl City)

18   Three little _ _ _ _ (Green Jelly)

19   Disco _ _ _ _ (Rick Dees)

20   Three _ _ _ _ _ (Baddiel, Skinner and the Lightning Seeds)

LIVIN' THING No.5

Answers

1 Monkey.
2 Hounds.
3 Lobster.
4 Buffalo.
5 Rhino.
6 Pigeon.
7 Wolves.
8 Birds, Bees.
9 Panther.
10 Cat, pigeons.
11 Monkey.
12 Tigers.
13 Elephant.
14 Owl.
15 Blackbird.
16 Butterfly.
17 Fireflies.

WORDS No.12

Can you identify these famous songs from their opening lyrics:

1. It's getting near dawn. When lights close their tired eyes. I'll soon be with you ....

2. Hey, if we can solve any problem, then why do we lose so many tears ....

3. All my life, and the hereafter, I've never seen, seen one like you. You're a knife ....

4. I was born in the wagon of a travellin' show. My mama used to dance for the money they'd throw ....

5. As I walk in da shadow of death, sixteen men on a deadman's chest ....

6. Who can fly my heart like a bamboo kite, make it twirl and gyrate ...

7. Some girls love to run around, love to handle everything they see.....

8. Once I was seven years old my momma told me, go make yourself some friends .....

9. I have a picture pinned to my wall. An image of you and me and we're laughing ....

10. You've got that look again. The one I hoped I had when I was a lad ....

11. They asked me how I knew, my true love was true. I of course replied ...

12. It's amazing how you can speak right into my heart. Without saying a word ....

13. My baby's always dancin' and it wouldn't be a bad thing, but I don't get no lovin' .....

14. Yeah, breakfast at Tiffany's and bottles of bubbles. Girls with tattoos ....

15. Our life together is so precious together. We have grown, we have grown ...

16. As I was goin' over the Cork and Kerry mountains, I saw Captain Farrell ....

17. Sometimes I feel like I don't have a partner, sometimes I feel like my only friend .....

18. Baby, you've been going so crazy. Lately, nothing seems to be going right ....

19. Here's a little song I wrote, you might want to sing it note for note ....

20. Every night I'm there. I'm always there, she knows I'm there, and heaven knows ....

WORDS No.12

Answers

1. Sunshine of your love (Cream).
2. Every time you go away (Paul Young).
3. Beautiful monster (Ne-Yo).
4. Gypsies, tramps and thieves (Cher).
5. Say what you want (Texas).
6. Only you can (Fox).
7. She'd rather be with me (Turtles).
8. 7 years (Lukas Graham).
9. Hold me now (Thompson Twins).
10. For your babies (Simply Red).
11. Smoke gets in your eyes (Platters).
12. When you say nothing at all (Ronan Keating).
13. Blame it on the boogie (Jacksons).
14. 7 Rings (Ariana Grande).
15. (Just like) Starting over (John Lennon).
16. Whiskey in the jar (Thin Lizzy).
17. Under the bridge (Red Hot Chilli Peppers).
18. Sing (Travis).
19. Don't worry, be happy (Bobby McFerrin).
20. Eloise (Barry Ryan).

THE NAME GAME No.12

By what names are the following better known:

1. Birgit Dieckmann.
2. William McPhail.
3. Brenda Gail Gatzimos.
4. Charles Edwin Hatcher.
5. Deirdre Elaine Cozier.
6. Marta Marrero.
7. Graham David Fellows.
8. Kimberley Grigsby.
9. Henry John Deutchendorf.
10. Carol Hedges.
11. Dorothy Smith.
12. William Dale Fries.
13. Ora Denise Allen.
14. Ellas McDaniel.
15. Russell A. Roberts.
16. Gary Stephen Anderson.
17. Mary Christine Brockert.
18. William Michael Albert Broad.
19. Elgin Baylor Lumpkin.
20. Orhan Terzi.

THE NAME GAME No.12

Answers

1. Billie Ray Martin.
2. Scott Fitzgerald.
3. Crystal Gayle.
4. Edwin Starr.
5. Dee D. Jackson.
6. Martika.
7. Jilted John.
8. Kym Mazelle.
9. John Denver.
10. Billie Davis.
11. Patra.
12. C. W. McCall.
13. Denise LaSalle.
14. Bo Diddley.
15. Russ Abbot.
16. Angry Anderson.
17. Tina Marie.
18. Billy Idol.
19. Ginuwine.
20. DJ Quicksilver.

WHO ARE YOU? No.12

Which name is missing from these song titles?

1   _ _ _ _ of Arc (Orchestral Manoeuvres in the Dark)
2   Poor _ _ _ (Led Zeppelin)
3   _ _ _ _ _ _ _ _ _ _ (Hootie and the Blowfish)
4   Polythene _ _ _ (The Beatles)
5   _ _ _ _ _ _ _ _ _ (Perry Como)
6   _ _ _ _ _ Gunn (Duane Eddy)
7   Oh _ _ _ _ _ (Fleetwood Mac)
8   Hello, this is _ _ _ _ _ _ (Paul Evans)
9   _ _ _ _ _ _ _ (Dr Feelgood)
10 _ _ _ 's town (The Killers)
11 Hey, _ _ _ _ _ _ _ (Karel Fialka)
12 _ _ _ _ (Hot Chocolate)
13 Da doo _ _ _ _ _ _ (Crystals)
14 _ _ _ _ _ _ Jones (Michael Cox)
15 _ _ _ _ _ _ come home (Fine Young Cannibals)
16 Run _ _ _ _ _ _ _ run (Chuck Berry)
17 _ _ _ _ _ _ came back (Duane Eddy)
18 _ _ _ _ _ (Chris Rea)
19 Behind these _ _ _ _ _ eyes (Kelly Clarkson)
20 _ _ _ _ _ _ _ _ (Robbie Williams)

WHO ARE YOU? No.12

Answers

1	Joan.
2	Tom.
3	Hannah Jane.
4	Pam.
5	Tina Marie.
6	Peter.
7	Diane.
8	Joanie.
9	Roxette.
10	Sam.
11	Matthew.
12	Emma.
13	Ron, Ron.
14	Angela.
15	Johnny.
16	Rudolph.
17	Bonnie.
18	Julia.
19	Hazel.
20	Bruce Lee.

EMPTY SPACES No.13

Fill in the blanks to reveal musicians who have had chart hits:

1. V _ N _ A   _ H _ P _ R _
2. P _ U _   W _ L _ E _
3. K _ V _ N   _ U _ O _ P _
4. T _ T _ A _ A   _ L _
5. H _ R _ I _   H _ N _ O _ K
6. A _ E _ A _ D _ R   _ Y _ A _
7. C _ O _ A _ H   _ O _ G _ R _
8. S _ R _   B _ R _ I _ L _ S
9. J _ C _ I _   T _ E _ T
10. J _ M   _ E _ V _ S
11. C _ A _ L _ E   _ U _ H
12. P _ R _ Y   _ L _ D _ E
13. N _ N _ Y   _ I _ A _ R _
14. L _ U _ Y _   H _ L _
15. N _ A _ L   _ O _ A _
16. J _ M _ Y   _ U _ F _ N.
17. G _ E _ N   _ A _ E _ R _ S
18. K _ R _ N   _ O _ N _
19. R _ B _ N   _ H _ C _ E
20. E _ W _ N   _ T _ R _

EMPTY SPACES No.13

ANSWERS

1. Vonda Shepard.
2. Paul Weller.
3. Kevin Rudolph.
4. Tatyana Ali.
5. Herbie Hancock.
6. Alexander Rybak.
7. Clodagh Rodgers.
8. Sara Bareilles.
9. Jackie Trent.
10. Jim Reeves.
11. Charlie Puth.
12. Percy Sledge.
13. Nancy Sinatra.
14. Lauryn Hill.
15. Niall Horan.
16. Jimmy Ruffin.
17. Glenn Medeiros.
18. Karen Young.
19. Robin Thicke.
20. Edwin Starr.

MIX IT UP No.7

Can you unravel the anagrams to identify these hit making bands?

1. VIVIANS TRAMP SON
2. EEL STEW LASHER
3. NET OR LOUD PET
4. PINK PIMMS HANGS US
5. ASH TAN SUIT
6. LEND YEAST
7. I SEE RICH FILM
8. I MOAN ZONE BIT
9. I SLAG RAW PEPPER PEAR
10. COIN IN A SPIRIT SPUD
11. YET KENNY FOULS
12. MERE NET FOUL
13. SWEAR LIGHTER
14. AM BALD IN SEX CLUB
15. GOOD OLD HUN BANG
16. MONK NEAR RAPESEED MALL
17. I USED METAL AT WET FEET
18. SUIT TWO SINGERS
19. PRIVATE FRONT ON COIN
20. PROOF MILK SWEEPS

MIX IT UP No.7

Answers

1. TRANSVISION VAMP
2. STEALERS WHEEL
3. TENPOLE TUDOR
4. SMASHING PUMPKINS
5. UTAH SAINTS
6. STEELY DAN
7. CLIMIE FISHER
8. ZOMBIE NATION
9. WEE PAPA GIRL RAPPERS
10. CUPIDS INSPIRATION
11. LYTE FUNKY ONES
12. ELEMENTFOUR
13. WEATHERGIRLS
14. CLIMAX BLUES BAND
15. BLOODHOUND GANG
16. EMERSON LAKE AND PALMER
17. SWEET FEMALE ATTITUDE
18. SWING OUT SISTER
19. FAIRPORT CONVENTION
20. MIKE FLOWERS POPS

THERE'S A PLACE No.7

Which place name is missing from these song titles?

1   _ _ _ _ _ _ _ from the flames (Robbie Williams)

2   For _ _ _ _ _ _ only (Alice Cooper)

3   _ _ _ _ _ _ _ (Led Zeppelin)

4   _ _ _ _ _ _ _ style (Psy)

5   _ _ _ _ _ (Genesis)

6   _ _ _ _ _ _ _ _ cowboy (Mike Harding)

7   _ _ _ _ _ _ _ _ _ _ _ _ (Bill Wyman)

8   I took a pill in _ _ _ _ _ (Mike Posner)

9   _ _ _ _ _ _ _ _ _ (Herb Alpert)

10   _ _ _ _ _ _ _ _ moon (Connie Francis)

11   The _ _ _ _ _ _ _ (Human League)

12   _ _ _ _ _ _ _ _ _ _ (Kenny Ball)

13   North to _ _ _ _ _ _ (Johnny Horton)

14   _ _ _ _ _ _ _ _ _ city limits (Robbie Williams)

15   _ _ _ _ _ _ _ city (Tom Jones)

16   Come to _ _ _ _ _ _ _ _ _ _ _ _ (Style Council)

17   _ _ _ _ _ _ _ _ _ express (Crosby, Stlls and Nash)

18   Battle of _ _ _ _ _ _ _ _ _ _ (Lonnie Donegan)

19   The devil went down to _ _ _ _ _ _ _ (Charlie Daniels Band)

20   Bar _ _ _ _ _ (Pulp)

THERE'S A PLACE No.7

Answers

1. Phoenix.
2. Britain.
3. Kashmir.
4. Gangnam.
5. Congo.
6. Rochdale.
7. Rio de Janeiro.
8. Ibiza.
9. Jerusalem.
10. Carolina.
11. Lebanon.
12. Casablanca.
13. Alaska.
14. Knutsford.
15. Detriot.
16. Milton Keynes.
17. Marrakesh.
18. New Orleans.
19. Georgia.
20. Italia.

COMMON PEOPLE No.5

What do the following have in common?

1. Country life, Manifesto, For your pleasure, Flesh and blood, Stranded.
2. Tony Jackson, Mike Pender, John McNally, Chris Curtis, Frank Allen.
3. Beautiful day, Dog train, Belaruse, Just the one, Fantasy.
4. Olivia Newton-John, The Hollies, Shirley Bassy, Cockney Rebel, Cream.
5. Ally Brooke, Normani Kordei, Dinah Jane, Lauren Jauregui, Camila Cabello.
6. Rain dogs, Frank's wild years, Blood money, Bone machine, Mule variation.
7. Sam Bailey, Crazy world of Arthur Brown, 3 of a kind, Anita Ward, Partners in Kryme.
8. What can I do?, Radio, Would you be happier? Summer sunshine, Only when I sleep.
9. Never had a dream come true, Go let it out, Fill me in, Can't fight the moonlight, Don't call me baby.
10. Stuart Murdoch, Isobel Campbell, Richard Colburn, Sarah Martin, Mick Cooke.
11. Everybody move, Waterloo sunset, Too many walls, C'mon and get my love, Falling.
12. Joni Mitchell, Drake, Shawn Mendes, Alannah Miles, Neil Young.
13. Spare parts, Under the influence, On the level, In search of the fourth chord, Dog of two head.
14. Olly Murs, Grace Davies, Andy Abraham, Rebecca Ferguson, Ray Quinn.
15. Getting away with it, Disappointed, Forbidden city, Vivid, Get the message
16. Please please me, Summer holiday, West side story, Out of the Shadows, With the Beatles.
17. Face to face, The village green preservation society, Percy, Schoolboys in disgrace, Low budget.
18. Rod Clements, Ray Jackson, Alan Hull, Ray Laidlaw, Simon Cowe.
19. The chauffeur, Lonely in your nightmare, My own way, Hold back the rain, New religion.
20. Written in the stars, Pass out, Text from your ex, Girls like, Trampoline.

COMMON PEOPLE No.5

ANSWERS

1. They are all albums by Roxy Music.

2. They were all members of The Searchers.

3. They are all hit singles by The Levellers.

4. They have all had hits with George Harrison compositions - 'What is life', 'If I needed someone', 'Something', 'Here comes the sun', 'Badge' (co-written with Eric Clapton).

5. The were all members of Fifth Harmony.

6. They are all albums by Tom Waits.

7. They all reached No.1 with their one and only hit single.

8. They were all hit singles by The Corrs.

9. They were all at No.1 during 2000 - and each of them for one week only!

10. They were all members of Belle and Sebastian.

11. They were all hit singles for Cathy Dennis.

12. They were all born in Toronto, Canada.

13. They are all albums by Status Quo.

14. They all finished in second place on the X Factor.

15. They were all hit singles by Electronic.

16. They all topped the album charts in 1963 - and these were the only ones at No.1 for the whole year.

17. They were all albums by The Kinks.

18. They were all members of Lindisfarne.

19. They are all from the Duran Duran album 'Rio'.

20. They were all hit singles by, or featuring, Tinie Tempah.

TWO OF US No.5

Can you complete the names of these duos?

1. Pat and ?
2. Peter Sellers and ?
3. Ferrante and ?
4. Joe and ?
5. Layo and ?
6. Dave and Ansell ?
7. Laurel and ?
8. Mouth and ?
9. Pepsi and ?
10. R and J ?
11. Zig and ?
12. Charles and ?
13. McFadden and ?
14. Louchie Lou and ?
15. Gallagher and ?
16. Chase and ?
17. Daryl Hall and ?
18. Phats and ?
19. Shanks and ?
20. John Otway and ?

TWO OF US No.5

Answers

1. Mick.
2. Sophia Loren.
3. Teicher.
4. Jake.
5. Bushwacka!
6. Collins.
7. Hardy.
8. MacNeal.
9. Shirley.
10. Stone.
11. Zag.
12. Eddie.
13. Whitehead.
14. Michie One.
15. Lyle.
16. Status.
17. John Oates.
18. Small.
19. Bigfoot.
20. Wild Willy Barrett ..... but could also be 'Attila the Stockbroker'.

BLANK SPACE No.13

Fill in the blanks to reveal bands that have had chart hits:

1. P_I_T_R_ _I_T_R_
2. B_S_M_N_ J_X_
3. T_A_S_I_I_N _A_P
4. C_E_C_L _R_T_E_S
5. S_E_L_ D_N
6. L_B_R_Y _
7. S_E_L_R_ W_E_L
8. N_A_ A_D _H_ W_A_E
9. B_A_C_A_G_
10. U_A_ S_I_T_
11. L_V_N_ I_ A _O_
12. O_E_L_N_E_S
13. H_T _H_P
14. C_A_N_M_K_R_
15. S_N_Y _N_ C_E_
16. C_P_A_N _K_
17. D_V_ D_E _O_Y _E_K_ M_C_ A_D _I_H
18. A_I_E _N _H_I_S
19. C_I_I_ F_S_E_
20. W_E_ P_P_ G_R_ R_P_E_S

BLANK SPACE No.13

ANSWERS

1. Pointer Sisters.
2. Basement Jaxx.
3. Transvision Vamp.
4. Chemical Brothers.
5. Steely Dan.
6. Liberty X.
7. Stealers Wheel.
8. Noah and the Whale.
9. Blancmange.
10. Utah Saints.
11. Living in a Box.
12. Overlanders.
13. Hot Chip.
14. Chainsmokers.
15. Sonny and Cher.
16. Captain Ska.
17. Dave Dee, Dozy, Beaky, Mick and Tich.
18. Alice in Chains.
19. Climie Fisher.
20. Wee Papa Girl Rappers.

LUCKY NUMBER No.7

Which cardinal or ordinal numbers are missing from these song titles?

1	_____ _____ _____ is a joke (Public Enemy)
2	Walk like a panther ' _____ (Tony Christie)
3	Quarter to _____ (Gary U S Bonds)
4	_____ little pigs (Green Jelly)
5	Land of _____ dances (Wilson Pickett)
6	_____ hearts (Kylie Minogue)
7	The magnificent _____ (John Barry)
8	_____ (James Blunt)
9	Richard _____ (Supergrass)
10	_____ times (Ann Lee)
11	Party fears _____ (Associates)
12	Just who is the _____ o'clock hero (Jam)
13	_____ - _____ (Connells)
14	Party fears _____ (Associates)
15	_____ in a _____ (S Club 7)
16	Theme _____ (Cozy Powell)
17	_____ - _____ (was my number) (Aswad)
18	Love plus _____ (Haircut One Hundred)
19	_____ , _____ , _____ (Dina Carroll)
20	The return of the Las Palmas _____ (Madness)

LUCKY NUMBER No.7

Answers

1   Nine, one, one.
2   Ninety eight.
3   Three.
4   Three.
5   One thousand.
6   Two.
7   Seven.
8   Nineteen seventy three (1973).
9   Third (III).
10 Two.
11 Two.
12 Five.
13 Seventy four, seventy five.
14 Two.
15 Two, million.
16 One.
17 Fifty four, forty six.
18 One.
19 One, two, three.
20 Seven.

WORDS No.13

Can you identify these famous songs from their opening lyrics:

1. It's a bit early in the midnight hour for me, to go through all the things tha I wanna be ....

2. It's nine o'clock on a Saturday, the regular crowd shuffles in ....

3. In Napoli where love is king, when boy meets girl here's what they say. When the moon hits your eye like a big pizza ....

4. Remember those walls I built, well baby, they're tumbling down ....

5. If there's anything you need, all you have to do is say. You know you satisfy ....

6. I'd tell myself you don't mean a thing. But what we got, got no hold on me ...

7. Left a good job in the city. Workin' for the man ev'ry night and day.....

8. You'll remember me when the west wind moves upon the fields of barley .....

9. Was the dark of the moon on the sixth of June in a Kenworth pullin' logs ....

10. Here, when all my work is done, she calls and she says, dear, can I come ....

11. Imagine me and you, I do. I think about you day and night, it's only right ....

12. When the snowman brings the snow, well, he just might like to know ....

13. Stop, slow down, take a deep breath (ooh yeah). Stop, slow down .....

14. Uno, dos, tres, cuatro. Yeah, oh baby, oh girl, oh lady, come to, come to me ....

15. Inside everyone hides one desire, outside no one would know ...

16. When I was just a little baby, I didn't have many toys. But, my mama used to say ....

17. I'm not proud. I was wrong and the truth is hard to take. I felt sure we had enough .....

18. Oh, angel sent you from above, you know you make my world light up ....

19. Take a look at my girlfriend, she's the only one I got. Not much of a girlfriend ....

20. It's a sign of the times, girl. Sad songs on the radio. It's a sign of the times ....

WORDS No.13

Answers

1. All around the world (Oasis).
2. Piano man (Billy Joel).
3. That's amore (Dean Martin).
4. Halo (Beyonce).
5. Together forever (Rick Astley).
6. Only love can hurt like this (Paloma Faith).
7. Proud Mary (Creedence Clearwater Revival).
8. Fields of gold (Sting).
9. Convoy (CW McCall).
10. Walk right now (Jacksons).
11. Happy together (Turtles).
12. I wish it could be Christmas every day (Wizzard).
13. A mind of its own (Victoria Beckham).
14. Why can't I wake up with you? (Take That).
15. We close our eyes (Go West).
16. Lucky Lips (Cliff Richard).
17. Lessons in love (Level 42).
18. Hymn for the weekend (Coldplay).
19. Breakfast in America (Supertramp).
20. Isn't it a wonder (Boyzone).

THE NAME GAME No.13

By what names are the following better known:

1. Delroy Easton McLean.
2. Alicia Augello Cook.
3. DeAndre Cortez Way.
4. Audrey Faith McGraw.
5. Alfred Jesse Smith.
6. Wasalu Muhammad Jaco.
7. Paul Spencer.
8. Jacqueline Nora Flood.
9. Jay Wayne Jenkins.
10. Eunice Kathleen Waymon.
11. Harold Ray Ragsdale.
12. Rowan John Harrington.
13. Josiane Grizeau.
14. Rowan Tyler Jones.
15. Priscilla Marie Veronica White.
16. Roland Kent LaVoie.
17. Dennis Princewell Stehr.
18. Patricia Jacqueline Sibley.
19. Egbert Nathaniel Dawkins.
20. Clementine Dinah Bullock.

THE NAME GAME No.13

Answers

1. Bitty McLean.
2. Alicia Keys.
3. Soulja Boy.
4. Faith Hill.
5. Brenton Wood.
6. Lupe Fiasco.
7. Dario G.
8. Jackie Lee.
9. Jeezy.
10. Nina Simone.
11 Ray Stevens.
12. Secondcity.
13. Severine.
14. Route 94.
15. Cilla Black.
16. Lobo.
17. Mr Probz.
18. Anne Shelton.
19. Aloe Blacc.
20. Cleo Laine.

ALL SHOOK UP No.7

Can you unravel the anagrams to identify these music personalities?

1. WASH ROD MAT
2. NOTE IT BRIAN
3. FISH ROD CAR CHART
4. ASIAN RODS
5. JEN SOLD NOEL
6. MORE ALE MOB
7. STEEP RED TARTS
8. RUN FALLEN MAFIA HIT
9. BATTER HUN
10. TRIED BED BAIT
11. FRY ON A VINE
12. CECIL PARTON
13. SAID STALL FINES
14. ROSE MARCH BYE
15. US MODERN MAN
16. SLY ANN ON NERD
17. DEAR SIR BORING
18. KEY RAVE SIN
19. RUDE WARP DIES
20. BELT PALE TAIL

ALL SHOOK UP No.7

Answers

1. WARD THOMAS
2. BONNIE RAITT
3. RICHARD ASHCROFT
4. DIANA ROSS
5. DONELL JONES
6. MELBA MOORE
7. PETER SARSTEDT
8. MARIANNE FAITHFULL
9. TAB HUNTER
10. EDDIE RABBITT
11. YVONNE FAIR
12. ERIC CLAPTON
13. LISA STANSFIELD
14. HARRY SECOMBE
15. DONNA SUMMER
16. LYNN ANDERSON
17. BORIS GARDINER
18. KEVIN AYRES
19. RUPIE EDWARDS
20. PATTI LABELLE

EMPTY SPACES No.14

Fill in the blanks to reveal musicians who have had chart hits:

1. R_B_C_A _H_A_L_Y
2. B_I_N _Y_A_D
3. L_N_A _E_I_
4. S_E_H_N _A_E_Y
5. J_S_I_ H_Y_A_D
6. L_S_ L_P_Z
7. C_R_S _N_R_W_
8. J_H_N_ B_I_T_L
9. J_S_I_A _I_P_O_
10. A_I_O_ L_M_R_C_
11. S_M_N W_B_E
12. S_R_H _H_T_O_E
13. S_N_H_N_ A_D_R_O_
14. B_D_Y _R_W_ B_Y
15. F_A_K_E _A_N_
16. C_N_Y _U_F_R.
17. J_M_S _Y_E
18 G_E_ C_M_B_L_
19. C_L_N_ D_O_
20. D_R_T_Y _O_R_

EMPTY SPACES No.14

ANSWERS

1. Rebecca Wheatley.
2. Brian Hyland.
3. Linda Lewis.
4. Stephen Gately.
5. Justin Hayward.
6. Lisa Lopez.
7. Chris Andrews.
8. Johnny Bristol.
9. Jessica Simpson.
10. Alison Limerick.
11. Simon Webbe.
12. Sarah Whatmore.
13. Sunshine Anderson.
14. Badly Drawn Boy.
15. Frankie Laine.
16. Candy Dulfer.
17. James Hype.
18. Glen Campbell.
19. Celine Dion.
20. Dorothy Moore.

WHO ARE YOU? No.13

Which name is missing from these song titles?

1. Sorry _____ (The Hollies)
2. ____ Malone (Teresa Brewer)
3. _____ Ocean (Undertones)
4. Looking for _____ (Hue and Cry)
5. ____ Queen of Nebraska (Bruce Springsteen)
6. _____ (Don Partridge)
7. ____ and _____ are dead (George Michael)
8. The house that ____ built (Alan Price)
9. _____ (Focus)
10. _____ the moocher (Cab Calloway)
11. I'm _____ fly me (10cc)
12. ____, pretty ballerina (Abba)
13. Ballad of Sir _____ Crisp (let it roll) (George Harrison)
14. _____'s mum (Fountains of Wayne)
15. Hey there _____ (Plain White T's)
16. _____ _____ Patterson's pet pig porky (The Monkees)
17. The wind cries ____ (Jimi Hendrix)
18. _____ & me (Hanson)
19. Dirty _____ (Gorillaz)
20. _____'s eyes (Nik Kershaw)

WHO ARE YOU? No.13

Answers

1	Suzanne.

2	Nora.

3	Julie.

4	Linda.

5	Mary.

6	Rosie.

7	John, Elvis.

8	Jack.

9	Sylvia.

10	Minnie.

11	Mandy.

12	Nina.

13	Frankie.

14	Stacy.

15	Delilah.

16	Peter, Percival.

17	Mary.

18	Penny.

19	Harry.

20	Elizabeth.

HAPPY BIRTHDAY No.7

Can you identify these musicians?

1. Singer born in Accrington, England on 30 July 1991.
2. Singer and pianist born in Waterford, Ireland on 1 December 1946.
3. Singer born in Atlanta, USA on 15 July 1952.
4. Keyboard player and singer born in Oxford, England on 2 June 1976.
5. Singer born in Cojimar, Cuba on 3 March 1997.
6. Singer born in Brynmawr, Wales on 10 October 1985.
7. Singer born in Newton-le-Willows, England on 6 February 1966.
8. Drummer and TV presenter born in Elderslie, Scotland on 15 October 1966.
9. Guitarist born in London, England on 9 March 1945.
10. Singer born in Grand Prairie, Texas, USA on 22 July 1992.
11. Singer born in Toronto, Canada on 8 August 1998.
12. DJ and musician born in Lymington, England on 4 December 1967.
13. Singer born in Pristina, Yugoslavia on 26 November 1990.
14. Singer and bassist born in West Bromwich, England on 20 August 1949.
15. Guitarist born in Ballyshannon, Ireland on 2 March 1948.
16. Singer and TV star born in Fort Worth, USA on 24 April 1982.
17. Flautist and singer born in Dunfermline, Scotland on 10 August 1947.
18. Singer born in Stone Town, Zanzibar on 5 September 1946.
19. Singer born in Melbourne, Florida, USA on 8 December 1943.
20. Singer born in Rugby, England on 13 August 1984.

HAPPY BIRTHDAY No.7

Answers

1. Diana Vickers.
2. Gilbert O'Sullivan.
3. Porter Robinson.
4. Tim Rice-Oxley.
5. Camila Cabello.
6. Marina (and the Diamonds).
7. Rick Astley.
8. Dougie Vipond.
9. Robin Trower.
10. Selena Gomez.
11. Shawn Mendes.
12. Adamski.
13. Rita Ora.
14. Phil Lynott.
15. Rory Gallagher.
16. Kelly Clarkson.
17. Ian Anderson.
18. Freddy Mercury.
19. Jim Morrison.
20. James Morrison.

JOIN TOGETHER No.6

These groups were known for backing which musician?

1. The Wailers.
2. The Whalers.
3. The Machine.
4. The Dinosaurs.
5. The Melody Makers.
6. The Pharohs.
7. Miami Sound Machine.
8. The Replays.
9. The Christmas Trees.
10. The Smurfs.
11. The Destroyers.
12. The Chipmunks.
13. The Drells.
14. The Medicine Show.
15. His Playboy Band.
16. The Sex-O-Lettes.
17. The Blowfish.
18. The Juniors.
19. The Hands of Dr Teleny.
20. The Wurzels.

JOIN TOGETHER No.6

Answers

1. Bob Marley.
2. Hal Paige.
3. Florence (Welch).
4. Terry Dactyl.
5. Ziggy Marley.
6. Sam the Sham.
7. Gloria Estifan.
8. Rocky Sharpe.
9. Santa Claus.
10. Father Abraham.
11. George Thorogood.
12. Alvin - or David Seville.
13. Archie Bell.
14. Dr Hook.
15. John Fred.
16. Disco-Tex.
17. Hootie.
18. Danny (Rapp).
19. Peter Straker.
20. Adge Cutler.

ANY COLOUR YOU LIKE No.5

Which colour is missing from these song titles?

1. Eyes of _____ (Paul Carrack)
2. _____ lady (David Soul)
3. The _____ shoes (Kate Bush)
4. _____ angel (Mica Paris)
5. Pretty in _____ (Psychedelic Furs)
6. Spin the _____ circle (Pearl Jam)
7. Cherry _____ and apple blossom _____ (Perez Prado)
8. _____ onions (Booker T)
9. Deeper shade of _____ (Steps)
10. _____ and _____ (Sam Sparro)
11. Don't it make my _____ eyes _____ (Crystal Gayle)
12. _____ hill (Coldplay)
13. _____ river (Christie)
14. _____ savannah (Erasure)
15. _____ light (Roll Deep)
16. a _____ sport coat (and a _____ carnation) (King Brothers)
17. The man in _____ (Cozy Powell)
18. _____ dream machine (David Essex)
19. Charlie _____ (The Coasters)
20. _____ alert (Basement Jaxx)

ANY COLOUR YOU LIKE No.5

Answers

1   Blue.
2   Silver.
3   Red.
4   Black.
5   Pink.
6   Black.
7   Pink, white.
8   Green.
9   Blue.
10 Black, gold.
11 Brown, blue.
12 Violet.
13 Yellow.
14 Blue.
15 Green.
16 White, pink.
17 Black.
18 Silver.
19 Brown.
20 Red.

ABC No.3

The letters of the names of these groups have been arranged in alphabetical order. can you identify them?

1. ABBCEHOSY.
2. ACHILMOSTUUY.
3. AACDEFS.
4. AADHMNOPPSYY.
5. ACEEGHLMORSSSY.
6. AAIIMNNOPRSSTVV.
7. AAACILNRRSTTT.
8. AEHIMNORSSTU.
9. CEEOORRSY.
10. AACEILMMPRRS.
11. AAEEFFORRRSST.
12. BEEHILORRSSTY.
13. AAACHIILSSTT.
14. ADEEGNRY.
15. ADDEEFLPPR.
16. AACDEEFIKLRVV.
17. ACCDEKSUU.
18. EENOORSSST.
19. ABCEEINRRRS.
20. EEGNOUV.

ABC No.3

Answers

1. Beach Boys.
2. Musical Youth.
3. Sad Cafe.
4. Happy Mondays.
5. Gym Class Heroes.
6. Transvision Vamp.
7. Atlantic Starr.
8. Housemartins.
9. Rose Royce.
10. Primal Scream.
11. Tears For Fears.
12. Isley Brothers.
13. Alicia's Attic.
14. Green Day.
15. Def Leppard.
16. Dave Clark Five.
17. Duck Sauce.
18. Stone Roses.
19. Cranberries.
20. En Vogue.

WOULD I LIE TO YOU? No.6

Are the following statements true or false?

1. Adele's first TV appearance was on Top of the Pops in 2006.

2. Despite releasing more than 50 singles, Aerosmith have only had four Top Ten hits in the UK.

3. Lulu was once married to Robin Gibb of the Bee Gees.

4. Beyonce's 2013 world tour was called 'The Mrs Brown Show'.

5. Brenda Lee was known as 'Little Miss Dynamite'.

6. Jim Morrison of the Doors died (and is buried) in Amsterdam aged 29.

7. 'Unchained melody' is the only song to have four different versions in the Top 20 at the same time.

8. Naomi Lynch of Buffalo G, is the sister of Edele and Keavy Lynch of B*Witched and Shane Lynch of Boyzone.

9. Dionne Warwick was the aunt of Whitney Houston.

10. The Four Tops released three hit singles before the Temptations had their first UK hit.

11. All members of the group Kings of Leon have the surname Followill.

12. Lindisfarne re-made their hit 'fog on the Tyne' in 1990 which featured Kevin Keegan.

13. Rod Stewart is the un-credited singer on Python Lee Jackson's 'In a broken dream'.

14. Professor Brian Cox was the keyboard player in both D-Ream and Dare.

15. Status Quo released 32 studio albums from 1968 until 2016.

16. Angelo Mysterioso is an alias sometimes used by Ed Sheeran.

17. Althea and Donna's No.1 hit 'Uptown top ranking' was recorded as a joke, but got numerous requests on radio after being played by accident by Mike Read.

18. Phil Spector, Jade Thirwall and Jay Farrar were all born on Boxing Day.

19. Evelyn King, Mariah Carey and The Monkees have all released an album titled 'Music Box'.

20. 'Baby come back' was a No.1 hit for The Tremeloes in 1967.

WOULD I LIE TO YOU? No.6

Answers

1. False - it was on 'Later ... with Jools Holland' in 2007.
2. False - they have only had one ('I don't want to miss a thing' in 1998).
3. False - it was Maurice Gibb that she married.
4. False - it was 'The Mrs Carter Show'.
5. True.
6. False - it was Paris, and he was 27.
7. True (Al Hibbler, Liberace, Les Baxter and Jimmy Young).
8. True.
9. False - they were cousins.
10. False - The Temptations had their first UK hit in 1964, the Four Tops in 1965.
11. True - they are brothers Caleb, Jared and Nathan, along with their cousin Matthew.
12. False - it was with Paul Gascoigne.
13. True.
14. True - he did play with both bands.
15. True.
16. True.
17. False - almost true, but it was John Peel and not Mike Read.
18. True - but in different years!
19. True.
20. False - it was a No.1 for The Equals in 1968.

BLANK SPACE No.14

Fill in the blanks to reveal bands that have had chart hits:

1. S _ I _ L _ Y   _ N _   C _ M _ A _ Y
2. L _ T _   F _ N _ Y   _ N _ S
3. C _ P _ D _   I _ S _ I _ A _ I _ N
4. V _ N _ A _ O _ S
5. Z _ M _ I _   N _ T _ O _
6. E _ E _ E _ T _ O _ R
7. A _   _ L _ C _   O _   S _ A _ U _ L _
8. D _ E _   D _ S _
9. A _ I _ N   _ N _   F _ R _
10. H _ R _ A _ S   _ E _ M _ T _
11. W _ E _ T _ S
12. C _ S _ I _   G _ T _
13. F _ A _ H   _ N _   P _ N
14. D _ N _ Y   _ O _ H _ L _
15. B _ O _ D _ O _ N _   G _ N _
16. T _ I _   L _ Z _ Y
17. S _ E _ T   _ E _ A _ E   _ T _ I _ U _ E
18. S _ A _ A _
19. A _ E _   P _ R _ Y
20. C _ E _ P   _ R _ C _

BLANK SPACE No.14

ANSWERS

1. Shirley and Company.
2. Lyte Funky Ones.
3. Cupids Inspiration.
4. Vengaboys.
5. Zombie Nation.
6. Elementfour.
7. A Flock of Seagulls.
8. Deep Dish.
9. Alien Ant Farm.
10. Herman's Hermits.
11. Wheatus.
12. Cosmic Gate.
13. Flash and the Pan.
14. Dandy Warhols.
15. Bloodhound Gang.
16. Thin Lizzy.
17. Sweet Female Attitue.
18. Shakaktak.
19. Alex Party.
20. Cheap Trick.

WORDS No.14

Can you identify these famous songs from their opening lyrics:

1. If I were to say to you 'Can you keep a secret?' Would you know just What to do ....

2. Here come old flat top, he come groovin' up slowly. He got joo joo eyeballs ....

3. As it grooves your body moves, your body starts to get the feelin' ....

4. I guess it's funnier from where you're standing 'cause from over here I miss the joke. Clear the way for my crash landing ....

5. Well, Billy rapped all night about his suicide, how he'd kick it in the head ....

6. When you move in right up close to me, that's when I get the shakes all over me ...

7. I had to escape. The city was sticky and cruel. Maybe I should have called you .....

8. He says he wants you. He says he needs you. It's real talking .....

9. There's no sign on the gate and there's mud on your face ....

10. If I could make a wish, I think I'd pass. Can't think of anything I'd need ....

11. White shirt now red, my bloody nose. Sleeping, you're on your tippy toes ....

12. This ain't no country club, and it ain't no disco. This is New York City ....

13. Sittin' here, eatin' my heart out waitin'. Waitin' for some lover to call .....

14. Ever since I was a young boy, I've played the silver ball. From Soho down to Brighton ....

15. Everything is wonderful. Being here is heavenly. Every single day ...

16. So, no one told you life was gonna be this way. Your job's a joke, you're broke ....

17. Ground Control to Major Tom, Ground Control to Major Tom .....

18. Years on the run, boy I know I can take it. And now that I'm here, I know you ....

19. Uh huh, make me tonight. Tonight make it right. Uh huh make me tonight ....

20. You keep saying you got something for me. Something you call love but confess ....

WORDS No.14

Answers

1. Poison arrow (ABC).
2. Come together (Beatles).
3. Wiggle it (2 in a Room).
4. Clown (Emili Sande).
5. All the young dudes (Mott the Hoople).
6. Shakin' all over (Johnny Kidd).
7. I drove all night (Cyndi Lauper).
8. Dip it low (Christina Milian).
9. Big mistake (Natalie Imbruglia).
10. The air that I breathe (Hollies).
11. Bad guy (Billie Eilish).
12. All I wanna do (Sheryl Crow).
13. Hot stuff (Donna Summer).
14. Pinball wizard (Who).
15. Mary's prayer (Danny Wilson).
16. I'll be there for you (Rembrandts).
17. Space Oddity (David Bowie).
18. Rock steady (All Saints).
19. Atomic (Blondie).
20. These boots are made for walking (Nancy Sinatra).

THERE'S A PLACE No.8

Which place name is missing from these song titles?

1. White cliffs of _ _ _ _ _ (Acker Bilk)
2. _ _ _ _ _ _ _ sky (China Crisis)
3. One night in _ _ _ _ _ _ _ (Murray Head)
4. _ _ _ _ _ _ (Kelly Clarkson)
5. _ _ _ _ - _ _ - _ _ _ _ _ _ (Winifred Atwell)
6. Miss _ _ _ _ _ _ _ _ (George Michael)
7. _ _ _ _ _ _ _ normals (Robbie Williams)
8. Miss _ _ _ _ _ _ _ (Blur)
9. _ _ _ _ _ _ _ _ blues (Hoagy Carmichael)
10. _ _ _ _ _ _ _ (Jimmy Cliff)
11. Mary, Queen of _ _ _ _ _ _ _ _ (Bruce Springsteen)
12. _ _ _ _ _ _ _ farewell (Harry Belafonte)
13. I left my heart in _ _ _ _ _ _ _ _ _ _ _ (Tony Bennett)
14. _ _ _ _ _ _ _ _ _ (Matthews Southern Comfort)
15. The _ _ _ _ _ _ _ _ _ grinder (Tony Capstick)
16. Way down yonder in _ _ _ _ _ _ _ _ _ _ (Freddy Cannon)
17. _ _ _ _ _ _ _ 's irie (Black Grape)
18. _ _ _ _ _ _ comma (Vampire Weekend)
19. _ _ _ _ _ _ _ (Prodigy)
20. Hey _ _ _ _ _ _ _ _ _ ! (Prefab Sprout)

THERE'S A PLACE No.8

Answers

1   Dover.

2   Arizona.

3   Bangkok.

4   Irvine.

5   Port - Au - Prince.

6   Sarajevo.

7   Burslem.

8   America.

9   Hong Kong.

10 Vietnam.

11 Arkansas.

12 Jamaica.

13 San Francisco.

14 Woodstock.

15 Sheffield.

16 New Orleans.

17 England.

18 Oxford.

19 Jericho.

20 Manhattan.

ALPHABET No.3

The letters of the names of these recording artists have been arranged in alphabetical order. can you identify them?

1. AACDLMMNOR.

2. AADEIMNNRT.

3. AADEILRSSY.

4. CEEEINNNOSSTV.

5. AACEIIKLSY.

6. AEEGGHINOORRRS.

7. AAACEHINRRY.

8. ACNORSSUWY.

9. AEEMMNTTTWYY.

10. BEHIILLRSTW.

11 AAGMNNRUY.

12. AADELNORTYY.

13. ADEEGILNNNOO.

14. AAELNPSU.

15. EEGIIKLMNOUY.

16. ADEEEHINO.

17. CEGIIRRSSSTTU.

18. AACDEJNOS.

19. BEEHIIIILLLS.

20. EJMNOOST.

ALPHABET No.3

Answers

1. Marc Almond.
2. Dean Martin.
3. Alyssa Reid.
4. Connie Stevens.
5. Alicia Keys.
6. George Harrison.
7. Mariah Carey.
8. Russ Conway.
9. Tammy Wynette.
10. Bill Withers.
11. Gary Numan.
12. Taylor Dayne.
13. Lonnie Donegan.
14. Sean Paul.
15. Kylie Minogue.
16. Headie One.
17. Curtis Stigers.
18. John Secada.
19. Billie Eilish.
20. Tom Jones.

THE NAME GAME No.14

By what names are the following better known:

1. Flora Yvonne Coleman.
2. Barry Authors.
3. Gasperino Cini.
4. Tiffany Cobb.
5. Louis Sharpe.
6. Rexton Rawlston Fernando Gordon.
7. Barry Ian Green.
8. Carol Joan Klein.
9. Marvin Burns.
10. Frederick Leslie Fowell.
11. Beatrice Melba Hill.
12. Jyoti Prakash Mishra.
13. Alexander Minto Hughes.
14. Alison Moira Clarkson.
15. Colin Trevor Flooks.
16. Timothy Lee McKenzie.
17. Shirley Klaris Yonavieve Edwards.
18. Andrew Youkim.
19. Joseph Edgar Forman.
20. Nana Richard Abiona.

THE NAME GAME No.14

Answers

1. Yvonne Fair.
2. J J Barrie.
3. Al Martino.
4. Blu Cantrell.
5. K7 (aka Kayel).
6. Shabba Ranks.
7. Barry Blue.
8. Carole King.
9. Lil Louis.
10. Freddie Starr.
11 Melba Moore.
12. White Town.
13. Judge Dread.
14. Betty Boo.
15. Cozy Powell.
16. Labrinth.
17. Skye.
18. Andy Kim.
19. Afroman.
20. Fuse ODG.

TWO OF US No.6

Can you complete the names of these duos?

1. Patience and ?
2. Trevor and ?
3. John Dummer and ?
4. Jan and ?
5. Shanks and ?
6. McAlmont and ?
7. Jazzy Jeff and ?
8. Letitia Dean and ?
9. De Etta Little and ?
10. Blank and ?
11. Rio and ?
12. Jet Harris and ?
13. Heller and ?
14. Frank and Nancy ?
15. Alan Braxe and ?
16. Quentin and ?
17. Edward Byrnes and ?
18. Eric B and ?
19. Santo and ?
20. Adam Clayton and ?

TWO OF US No.6

Answers

1. Prudence.
2. Simon (Neal and Hickson).
3. Helen April.
4. Dean ..... but could also be 'Kjeld'.
5. Bigfoot.
6. Butler.
7. The Fresh Prince.
8. Paul Medford.
9. Nelson Pigford.
10. Jones.
11. Mars.
12. Tony Meehan.
13. Farley.
14. Sinatra.
15. Fred Falke.
16. Ash (Caroline and Lesley).
17. Connie Stevens.
18. Rakim.
19. Johnny.
20. Larry Mulligan.

EMPTY SPACES No.15

Fill in the blanks to reveal musicians who have had chart hits:

1. D _ A   L _ P _
2. S _ I _ L _ Y   _ L _ I _
3. A _ Y   _ A _ D _ N _ L _
4. G _ R _ O _   H _ S _ E _ L
5. S _ A _ E _   S _ L _ M _ N
6. A _ G _ Y   _ N _ E _ S _ N
7. B _ R _ A _ A   _ I _ K _ O _
8. D _ N _ L _   J _ N _ S
9. B _ N _ I _   R _ I _ T
10. E _ D _ E   _ A _ B _ T _
11. L _ O _   J _ C _ S _ N
12. J _ N _ I _ E _   R _ S _
13. S _ A _ M _ N   _ O _ N
14. V _ N _ S _ A   _ M _ R _ S _
15. M _ R _ A _ N _   F _ I _ H _ U _ L
16. R _ P _ E   _ D _ A _ D _
17. P _ I _ C _   B _ S _ E _
18 J _ D _ E   _ R _ A _
19. S _ S _ N   _ A _ O _ A _
20. D _ V _   E _ M _ N _ S

EMPTY SPACES No.15

ANSWERS

1. Dua Lipa.
2. Shirley Ellis.
3. Amy MacDonald.
4. Gordon Haskell.
5. Stacey Solomon.
6. Angry Anderson.
7. Barbara Dickson.
8. Donell Jones.
9. Bonnie Raitt.
10. Eddie Rabbitt.
11. Leon Jackson
12. Jennifer Rush.
13. Scatman John.
14. Vanessa Amorosi.
15. Marianne Faithfull.
16. Rupie Edwards.
17. Prince Buster.
18. Judge Dread.
19. Susan Cadogan.
20. Dave Edmunds.

WHO ARE YOU? No.14

Which name is missing from these song titles?

1 _ _ _ _ _ 's heroes (Black Grape)
2 The continuing story of bungalow _ _ _ _ (The Beatles)
3 _ _ _ _ _ and the wolf (Clyde Valley Stompers)
4 Amazing _ _ _ _ _ (Judy Collins)
5 _ _ _ _ _ _ (Laura Branigan)
6 _ _ _ _ _ _ (Pearl Jam)
7 _ _ _ _ _ _ _ _ (all night long) (Mary J Blige)
8 The ballad of _ _ _ Jones (Space with Cerys)
9 _ _ _ _ _ hold on (B*Witched)
10 _ _ _ _ _ _ (Bjork)
11 I was Kaiser _ _ _ _ 's batman (Whistling Jack Smith)
12 _ _ _ _ _ _ _ (Black Lace)
13 _ _ _ _ _ _ _ _ (Nick Cave)
14 _ _ _ _ _ 's theme from 'Limelight' (Frank Chacksfield)
15 Little _ _ _ _ _ (Oasis)
16 _ _ _ _ _ _ and _ _ _ _ (Robert Palmer)
17 _ _ _ _ _ _ _ _ (Perez Prado)
18 _ _ _ _ _ _ _ _ _ _ (Gene Pitney)
19 The ballad of _ _ _ _ Crockett (Tennessee Ernie Ford)
20 _ _ _ _ _ _ _ (Gibson Brothers)

WHO ARE YOU? No.14

Answers

1	Kelly.
2	Bill.
3	Peter.
4	Grace.
5	Gloria.
6	Jeremy.
7	Mary Jane.
8	Tom.
9	Jesse.
10	Isobel.
11	Bill.
12	Mary Ann.
13	Henry Lee.
14	Terry.
15	James.
16	Johnny, Mary.
17	Patricia.
18	Maria Elena.
19	Davy.
20	Mariana.

THE FIRST No.4

1. What was the title of David Bowie's first No.1 album?
2. 'We close our eyes' was the first hit for which duo?
3. What was the title of Oasis' first No.1 hit single?
4. Who was the first person to be No.1 in the UK and the USA at the same time?
5. What was the title of Ellie Goulding's first album?
6. Who was the first professional footballer to have a solo chart hit?
7. Whose first hit was 'The closest thing to crazy?
8. What was the title of Mike Oldfield's first No.1 album?
9. Who were the first father and daughter to top the charts both as solo artistes and together as a duo?
10. What was the first hit single by The Small Faces?
11. Whose first album was called 'I cry when I laugh'?
12. What was the first track on the album Disraeli Gears by Cream?
13. Who was the first person to leave Pink Floyd after they started releasing records?
14. Which group's first UK Top Twenty hit was 'I get around'?
15. 'Second hand news' is the first track on which Fleetwood Mac album?
16. What was the first hit single for the Everly Brothers?
17. 'Sing this altogether' is the first track on which Rolling Stones album?
18. Whose first hit was 'Fell in love with a boy'?
19. Colosseum's 'Valentyne Suite' was the first album released on what record label?
20. What was the title of Tears for Fears first UK No.1 album?

THE FIRST No.4

Answers

1. Aladdin Sane.
2. Go West.
3. Some might say.
4. David Whitfield.
5. Lights.
6. Kevin Keegan - with 'Head over heels in love' in 1979.
7. Katie Melua.
8. Hergest Ridge - and it was knocked off the top by 'Tubular Bells', his first album.
9. Frank and Nancy Sinatra - and to date, the only ones.
10. Whatcha gonna do about it?.
11. Jess Glynne.
12. Strange brew.
13. Syd Barrett.
14. Beach Boys.
15. Rumours.
16. Bye bye love.
17. Their Satanic Majesties Request.
18. Joss Stone.
19. Vertigo.
20. The Hurting.

MIX IT UP No.8

Can you unravel the anagrams to identify these hit making bands?

1. PRESS EMU
2. SHORT BREW RAP
3. RUN DADA RUN
4. SHUT OUT IF A BLUE
5. I DO LEAD RAVE
6. BREW AS TOY
7. NEED MY OLD GRACE
8. CASH IT AT ALI
9. SEE MY BRA SET
10. I PAY ONES CLASS RATIO
11. SEAL IN BEATLES BAND
12. SHUN FOR DOD
13. MASH ALE JO
14. SWING
15. OFF TOY IN ARCTIC
16. RAN AT MY RUDE APPLE
17. FORT OPUS
18. EAR FUSS SOON
19. FLY CAN DIP
20. CRAVE RUDI

MIX IT UP No.8

Answers

1. SUPREMES
2. WARP BROTHERS
3. DURAN DURAN
4. BEAUTIFUL SOUTH
5. DEAD OR ALIVE
6. WATERBOYS
7. GODLEY AND CREME
8. ALISHA'S ATTIC
9. MERSEYBEATS
10. PLAYERS ASSOCIATION
11. BELLE AND SEBASTIAN
12. HUDSON FORD
13. HALO JAMES
14. WINGS
15. FICTION FACTORY
16. PETER PAUL AND MARY
17. FOUR TOPS
18. FOUR SEASONS
19. CANDY FLIP
20. CURVED AIR

LIVIN' THING No.6

Which creatures are missing from these song titles?

1   _____ on the wire (Beautiful South)
2   Honey to the ___ (Billie Piper)
3   Ride a wild _____ (Dee Clark)
4   _____ suit (Paul Weller)
5   Solomon bites the ____ (Bluetones)
6   Pretty _____ (Manfred Mann)
7   ____ at the door (Keane)
8   Little ____ (Annie Lennox)
9   Holy ___ (Lee Dorsey)
10 Pickin' a _____ (Eve Boswell)
11 The ugly _____ (Mike Reid)
12 Live like _____ (Elton John and Luciano Pavarotti)
13 _____ were _____ (Ian Brown)
14 I'm like a ____ (Nelly Furtado)
15 ____ in the Heather (Sonic Youth)
16 Who let the ____ out? (Baha Men)
17 _____ (R-Kelly with Big Tigger)
18 Love me love my ___ (Peter Shelley)
19 She ____ (Shakira)
20 Free as a ____ (Beatles)

LIVIN' THING No.6

Answers

1   Blackbird.

2   Bee.

3   Horse.

4   Peacock.

5   Worm.

6   Flamingo.

7   Wolf.

8   Bird.

9   Cow.

10 Chicken.

11 Duckling.

12 Horses.

13 Dolphins, monkeys.

14 Bird.

15 Bull.

16 Dogs.

17 Snake.

18 Dog.

19 Wolf.

20 Bird.

BLANK SPACE No.15

Fill in the blanks to reveal bands that have had chart hits:

1. E _ E _ S _ N   _ A _ E   A _ D   _ A _ M _ R
2. K _ N   _ A _
3. C _ A _ H   _ E _ T   _ U _ M _ E _
4. W _ R _   B _ O _ H _ R _
5. D _ U _ L _   9 _
6. A _ T _ R   _ H _   F _ R _
7. K _ N _ S
8. F _ U _   T _ P _
9. M _ L _ K _ (only one letter required!)
10. X _   _ A _   S _ E _
11. B _ L _ E   _ N _   S _ B _ S _ I _ N
12. R _ C _ I _'   B _ R _ I _ S
13. J _ S _ S   _ O _ E _
14. K _ S _ I _ G   _ H _   P _ N _
15. H _ L _   J _ M _ S
16. A _ P _ E _ A _ K _
17. C _ I _ A _ O
18. A _ I _ H _ S   _ T _ I _
19. N _ W   E _ I _ I _ N
20. C _ O _ I _   C _ E _

BLANK SPACE No.15

ANSWERS

1. Emerson Lake and Palmer.
2. Kon Kan.
3. Crash Test Dummies.
4. Warp Brothers.
5. Double 99.
6. After the Fire.
7. Kinks.
8. Four Tops.
9. Moloko.
10. X Ray Spex.
11. Belle and Sebastian.
12. Rockin' Berries.
13. Jesus Jones.
14. Kissing the Pink.
15. Halo James.
16. Applejacks.
17. Chicago.
18. Alisha's Attic.
19. New Edition.
20. Cookie Crew.

WE ARE FAMILY No 4

Which human relations are missing from these song titles?

1 Never turn your back on _ _ _ _ _ _ Earth (Sparks)

2 My perfect _ _ _ _ _ _ (Undertones)

3 _ _ _ _ was a rollin' stone (Temptations)

4 Mr Manic and _ _ _ _ _ _ Cool (Shakatak)

5 _ _ _ _ _ _ stands for comfort (Kate Bush)

6 100 _ _ _ _ _ _ _ _ _ (Mac Miller)

7 A _ _ _ for a _ _ _ (Smashing Pumpkins)

8 Abraham's _ _ _ _ _ _ _ _ (Arcade Fire)

9 _ _ _ _ thing (Pixie Geldof)

10 Bob's yer _ _ _ _ _ (Happy Mondays)

11 _ _ _ _ _ _ Mary (UFO)

12 _ _ _ _ _ issues (Demi Lovato)

13 _ _ _ _ Lisa (Mastodon)

14 My _ _ _ _ _ _ had a _ _ _ _ _ _ _ (George Michael)

15 _ _ _ _ _ (Beyonce)

16 Coal miner's _ _ _ _ _ _ _ _ (Loretta Lynn)

17 Does your _ _ _ _ _ _ know (ABBA)

18 _ _ _ _ _ _ Dupree (Steey Dan)

19 Babylon _ _ _ _ _ _ _ (Steely Dan)

20 _ _ _ _ _ _ 's little helper (Rolling Stones).

WE ARE FAMILY No.4

Answers

1	Mother.
2	Cousin.
3	Papa.
4	Sister.
5	Mother.
6	Grandkids.
7	Son son.
8	Daughter.
9	Twin.
10	Uncle.
11	Mother.
12	Daddy.
13	Aunt.
14	Mother, brother.
15	Daddy.
16	Daughter.
17	Mother.
18	Cousin.
19	Sisters.
20	Mother.

WORDS No.15

Can you identify these famous songs from their opening lyrics:

1. I could stay awake just to hear you breathing. Watch you smile ....

2. Where have all the good men gone, and where are all the gods? ....

3. What would you do if I sang out of tune? Would you stand up and walk out ....

4. Spent 24 hours, I need more hours with you. You spent the weekend getting even ....

5. Every day I spend my time drinkin' wine, feelin' fine, waitin' here to find the sign ...

6. Like a warrior that fights and wins the battle, I know the taste of victory ...

7. Well, I told you once and I told you twice, but you never listen to my advice .....

8. I'd rather be liberated, I find myself captivated. Stop doing what you do .....

9. I talked to my baby on the telephone, long distance. I never would have guessed ....

10. Mmm, if the fish swam out of the ocean and grew legs and they started walking ....

11. Some boys kiss me, some boys hug me, I think they're okay. If they don't give me proper credit ....

12. Oh, the shark, babe, has such teeth, dear, and it shows them pearly white ....

13. You were my sun, you were my earth. But, you didn't know all the ways I loved .....

14. My baby moves at midnight, goes right on till the dawn. My woman takes me ....

15. Now, if you feel that you can't go on because all of your hope is gone ...

16. If we could see tomorrow, what are your plans? No one can live in sorrow ....

17. Outside another yellow moon has punched a hole in the night time mist .....

18. I've got your picture of me and you. I wrote 'I love you', you wrote 'me too' ....

19. Like a small boat on the ocean, sending big waves into motion ....

20. So long boy, you can take my place, got my papers, I've got my pay .....

WORDS No.15

Answers

1. I don't want to miss a thing (Aerosmith).
2. Holding out for a hero (Bonnie Tyler).
3. With a little help from my friends (Joe Cocker).
4. Girls like you (Maroon 5).
5. In a broken dream (Python Lee Jackson).
6. I knew you were waiting (for me) (George Michael and Aretha Franklin).
7. The last time (Rolling Stones).
8. Mulder and Scully (Catatonia).
9. Never let her slip away (Andrew Gold).
10. Black and gold (Sam Sparro).
11. Material girl (Madonna).
12. Mack the knife (Bobby Darin).
13. Cry me a river (Justin Timberlake).
14. You should be dancing (Bee Gees).
15. Reach out I'll be there (Four Tops).
16. Don't cry (Guns N' Roses).
17. Downtown train (Rod Stewart).
18. Turning Japanese (Vapors).
19. Fight song (Rachel Platten).
20. Yellow river (Christie).

THE NAME GAME No.15

By what names are the following better known:

1. Christopher Brian Bridges.
2. Siobhan Bethel.
3. Jermaine Scott Sinclair.
4. Concetta Kirschner.
5. Frank Abelson.
6. Juan Francisco Secada Ramirez.
7. Nicole Prescovia Elikolante.
8. Claire Mary Teresa Rawstron.
9. Josh Abrahams.
10. Helen Folasade Adu.
11 Elli David Fitoussi.
12. Norman Washington Giscombe.
13. Harold Lloyd Jenkins.
14. Christine Flores.
15. Nicholas Douwma.
16. James Gabriel Keogh.
17. Vassiliki Papathanasiou.
18. Roger McKenzie.
19. Sean Patrick Michael Sherrard.
20. Natasja de Witte.

THE NAME GAME No.15

Answers

1. Ludacris.
2. Joan Regan.
3. Wretch 32.
4. Princess Superstar.
5. Frankie Vaughan.
6. Jon Secada.
7. Nicole Scherzinger.
8. Kiri Te Kanawa.
9. Puretone - aka The Pagan and Bassliners.
10. Sade.
11. F R David.
12. Junior.
13. Conway Twitty.
14. Christina Milian.
15. Sub Focus.
16. Vance Joy.
17. Vicky Leandros.
18. Wildchild.
19. Johnny Logan.
20. Kira.

THERE'S A PLACE No.9

Which place name is missing from these song titles?

1	_ _ _ _ _ storm warning (Elvis Costello)
2	5am in _ _ _ _ _ _ _ (Drake)
3	6am in _ _ _ _ _ _ _ (Drake)
4	_ _ _ _ _ _ _ park (Prince)
5	_ _ _ _ _ _ _ _ _ (Guns N' Roses)
6	_ _ _ _ _ _ _ (Linda Scott)
7	Funkin' for _ _ _ _ _ _ _ (NY) (Tom Browne)
8	_ _ _ _ _ _ _ _ _ _ lassie (Freddy Cannon)
9	_ _ _ _ _ (Will SWmith)
10	Blue _ _ _ _ _ _ _ _ (Erasure)
11	_ _ _ _ _ _ (Marty Robbins)
12	A _ _ _ _ _ _ _ _ _ love thing (50 Cent)
13	_ _ _ _ _ _ _ _ (Red Hot Chilli Peppers)
14	Midnight in _ _ _ _ _ _ _ (Jon Bon Jovi)
15	_ _ _ _ _ _ _ _ _ _ _ _ _ _ (Future Sound of London)
16	From _ _ _ _ _ _ _ to _ _ (Patsy Gallant)
17	_ _ _ _ _ _ groove (Hello)
18	_ _ _ _ _ 2 _ _ _ _ _ (Swedish House Mafia)
19	When _ _ _ _ _ _ gave up the rumba (Mitchell Torok)
20	Left my heart in _ _ _ _ _ (Mini Viva)

THERE'S A PLACE No.9

Answers

1   Tokyo.
2   Toronto.
3   New York.
4   Paisley.
5   Madagascar.
6   Bermuda.
7   Jamaica.
8   Tallahassee.
9   Miami.
10   Savannah.
11   El Paso.
12   Baltimore.
13   Ethiopia.
14   Chelsea.
15   Papua New Guinea.
16   New York, LA.
17   New York.
18   Miami, Ibiza.
19   Mexico.
20   Tokyo.

YOU'RE THE ONE No. 5

Can you spot the odd one out in each case?

1. My everything, Dangerous woman, Sweetner, Yours truly, Always in between.
2. American hearts, Suddenly, Liberian girl, Loverboy, Calypso crazy.
3. Crazy World of Arthur Brown, Blind Faith, Ginger Baker's Air Force, Traffic, Spencer Davis Group.
4. The young ones, Moon river, Good luck charm, Come outside, Only sixteen.
5. The sound of music, Beauty school dropout, Your song, Come what may, El tango de Roxanne.
6. Betty Kelly, Florence Ballard, Mary Wilson, Jean Terrell, Cindy Birdsong
7. Talking book, Silk electric, Conversation peace, Innervisions, In square circle.
8. Can't stop the feeling! Rock your body, One less lonely girl, Take back the night, Like I love you.
9. Raindrops keep fallin' on my head, Surround yourself with sorrow, (There's) always something there to remind me, Twenty four hours from Tulsa, This guy's in love with you.
10. Tim Hauser, Janis Siegel, Paul Griggs, Cheryl Bentyne, Alan Paul.
11. Concrete and gold, Only by the night, Because of the times, Mechanical bull, Come around sundown.
12. Question, Amazing grace, Telstar, Eye level, Albatross.
13. Dancing Queen, The winner takes it all, Dum dum diddle, When I kissed the teacher, Knowing me knowing you.
14. Bonkers, Swagger Jagger, Run this town, sexy chick, Boom boom pow.
15. Drop the boy, So cold the night, Madly in love, Chocolate box, Cat among the pigeons.
16. Sweet talker, Music of the sun, Rated R, Talk that talk, Good girl gone bad.
17. John Lord, Roger Glover, Ian Paice, Ritchie Blackmore, Tony Iommi.
18. Dexy's Midnight Runners, Merton Parkas, Bronski Beat, Style Council, Boogie Box High.
19. Marion Raven, Cher, Patti Rousso, Lulu, Pearl Aday.
20 She's kinda hot, Kings and Queens, Up in the air, From yesterday, Closer to the edge.

YOU'RE THE ONE No 5

ANSWERS

1. Always in between - was an album by Jess Glynne, the other are Ariana Grande albums.

2. Liberian girl - was a hit single for Michael Jackson, the rest were hits for Billy Ocean.

3. Crazy World of Arthur Brown - Steve Winwood was not in this group, but he was a member of the other ones.

4. Only sixteen - was a No.1 from 1959, the others topped the chart in 1962.

5. Beauty school dropout - is from 'Grease', the others are sung by Ewan McGregor in 'Moulin Rouge'.

6. Betty Kelly - was with The Vandellas, the others were with The Supremes.

7. Silk electric - is an album by Diana Ross, the others are albums by Stevie Wonder.

8. One less lonely girl - was a hit single by Justin Bieber, the others were by Justin Timberlake.

9. Surround yourself with sorrow - was written by Bill Martin and Phil Coulter, the others were written by Burt Bacharach and Hal David.

10. Paul Griggs - was with Guys 'n' Dolls, the others were Manhattan Transfer.

11. Concrete and gold - is an album by the Foo Fighters, the others are Kings of Leon albums.

12. Question - was a No.2 hit song by the Moody Blues, the others were instrumentals that reached No.1.

13. The winner takes it all - is a track on Abba's 'Super trouper', the others are from Abba's 'Arrival'.

14. Swagger Jagger - was a No.1 hit from 2011, the others topped the chart in 2009.

15. So cold the night - was a hit single by The Communards, the others were by Bros.

16. Sweet talker - is an album by Jessie J, the others are albums by Rihanna.

17. Tony Iommi - was with Black Sabbath, the others were members of Deep Purple.

18. Bronski Beat - Mick Talbot was never in this group, but he was keyboard player in the others.

19. Lulu - has never had a hit with Meat Loaf, the others have had hits duet-ting with him.

20. She's kinda hot - was a hit single for 5 Seconds of Summer, the others were singles by 30 Seconds to Mars.

ALL SHOOK UP No.8

Can you unravel the anagrams to identify these music personalities?

1. PLUM BREEDER THEN KING
2. CRY POOR ME
3. IRON HASH PEEL
4. LOSE TOP MAN
5. EVIL AT DOOM
6. LONDON AGE NINE
7. FLY JEW CANE
8. GORY BAG TO BERT
9. NEW LARK DOLLY
10. CHASED A LIST
11. I SANG DRY FIRE
12. I TRUST VANDALS
13. A GINA LEE PIE
14. NAIL DIME GANG MEN
15. DEANE NOW WRY
16. A LINNEN OXEN
17. A TIN MAN RIVER WAR
18. SHORT AIR LAND
19. LEVEL SOIL COST
20. FUND SPY GIRLS DIET

ALL SHOOK UP No.8

Answers

1. ENGLEBERT HUMPERDINK
2. PERRY COMO
3. HELEN SHAPIRO
4. POST MALONE
5. DEMI LOVATO
6. LONNIE DONEGAN
7. WYCLEF JEAN
8. GREGORY ABBOTT
9. KELLY ROWLAND
10. SACHA DISTEL
11. FREYA RIDINGS
12. ALVIN STARDUST
13. ELAINE PAIGE
14. MAGGIE LINDEMANN
15. WAYNE WONDER
16. ANNIE LENNOX
17. MARVIN RAINWATER
18. DALTON HARRIS
19. ELVIS COSTELLO
20. DUSTY SPRINGFIELD

EMPTY SPACES No.16

Fill in the blanks to reveal musicians who have had chart hits:

1. S _ A _ N   _ E _ D _ S
2. C _ I _ D _ S _   G _ M _ I _ O
3. A _ I _   S _ E _ A _ T
4. J _ H _   N _ W _ A _
5. B _ I _ N   _ A _
6. A _ N _   S _ E _ T _ N
7. N _ N _   S _ M _ N _
8. A _ O _   B _ A _ C
9. J _ C _ I _   W _ L _ O _
10. J _ N _ O _   C _ M _ B _ L _
11. K _ L _ Y   _ S _ O _ R _ E
12. P _ I _ I _   G _ O _ G _
13. C _ E _   L _ I _ E
14. V _ N _ S _ A   _ I _ L _ A _ S
15. J _ S _ I _   T _ M _ E _ L _ K _
16. R _ F _ A _ L _ A   _ A _ R _
17. J _ M _ S   G _ L _ A _
18 J _ R _ A _ N _   S _ E _ A _ T
19. L _ U _ S _   J _ H _ S _ N
20. K _ N _ R _ C _   L _ M _ R

EMPTY SPACES No.16

ANSWERS

1. Shawn Mendes.
2. Childish Gambino.
3. Amii Stewart.
4. John Newman.
5. Brian May.
6. Anne Shelton.
7. Nina Simone.
8. Aloe Blacc.
9. Jackie Wilson.
10. Junior Campbell.
11. Kelly Osbourne.
12. Philip George.
13. Cleo Laine.
14. Vanessa Williams.
15. Justin Timberlake.
16. Raffaella Carra.
17. James Galway.
18. Jermaine Stewart.
19. Louisa Johnson.
20. Kendrick Lamar.

JOIN TOGETHER No.7

These groups were known for backing which musician?

1. The Living Bass.
2. The Shondells.
3. His Rockers.
4. The Johnson Brothers.
5. The Big Roll Band.
6. The Sabres.
7. The Tuxedo.
8. The Hot Rods.
9. The Vibrations.
10. The Buzzy Bunch.
11. The Devotions.
12. The Terminaters.
13. The Bad Seeds.
14. The Yellowcoats.
15. The Plastic Jam.
16. His 'Pops' Concert Orchestra.
17. The Big Family.
18. The Alfa-Beta.
19. Cockney Rebel.
20. The Chameleons.

JOIN TOGETHER No.7

Answers

1. Jay Mondi.
2. Tommy James.
3. Boyd Bennett.
4. Suzi Miller.
5. Zoot Money.
6. Danny Seyton.
7. Bobby Angelo.
8. Eddie (who, or rather which, in fact, was a dummy).
9. Tony Jackson.
10. Celi Bee (Celina Ines Camacho).
11. Belle.
12. Arnee.
13. Nick Cave.
14. Paul Shane.
15. Bug Kann.
16. Leroy Anderson.
17. J T.
18. Izhar Cohen.
19. Steve Harley.
20. Lori.

WOULD I LIE TO YOU? No.7

Are the following statements true or false?

1. Nancy Nova is the daughter of former Blockbusters presenter and DJ, Bob Holness.

2. Rod Stewart and Bradley Walsh both had trials with Crystal Palace FC.

3. Fragma's No.1 hit, 'Toca's miracle' was a mash up of their previous recording 'Toca me' and Coco Star's 'I need a miracle'.

4. Pamela Jayne Harvey is better known as PJ Harvey.

5. Graham Coxon is the drummer with Blur.

6. Bryan Ferry and Alan Price were both born in Washington, County Durham.

7. Despite releasing over 50 singles, Garth Brooks has had only one UK Top Ten hit.

8. The original line up of Bachman Turner Overdrive consisted of Fred Turner and three Bachman brothers.

9. 'The 20/20 experience' and 'Man of the woods' are albums by Justin Timberlake.

10. Dave Gilmour is the only person to have played on every Pink Floyd album.

11. Sam Cooke, John Lennon and Marvin Gaye all died by shooting.

12. Iron Maiden was founded in 1975 by bassist Steve Harris, who is the only original member still playing with the band.

13. Mick Jagger and Keith Richards are sometimes known as The Glitter Twins.

14. Both Bryan Adams and Ryan Adams were born on 5 November.

15. Gabrielle was born as Louisa Bobb.

16. Carl Palmer and Cozy Powell were drummers in two versions of the group 'ELP'.

17. Sandra Dee Olsson was the lead female role in the stage, film and TV versions of the popular musical, 'Grease'.

18. Despite releasing singles since 1951, it wasn't until 1955 that Little Richard had a chart hit.

19. Hawkwind released over 50 albums and 20 singles between 1970 and 2017.

20. 'Sugar baby love' was a No.1 hit for The Bay City Rollers in 1975.

WOULD I LIE TO YOU? No.7

Answers

1. True - as is Ros Holness from Toto Coelo.
2. False - it was Brentford FC, and Bradley was signed as a professional.
3. True.
4. False - PJ Harvey is Polly Jean Harvey.
5. Flase - he's a guitarist. Dave Rowntree is the drummer.
6. True.
7. False - he's never had a Top Ten hit, two Top 20 hits are his best chart positions.
8. True - Randy, Robbie and Tim Bachman.
9. True.
10. False - Nick Mason is the only one to have done this.
11. True.
12. True.
13. False - they're The Glimmer Twins.
14. True - but 15 years apart.
15. True - Gabrielle is her middle name.
16. True - both with Keith Emerson and Greg Lake.
17. False - only in the film version. She was Sandra Dumbrowski on stage and Sandy Young on TV.
18. True.
19. True.
20. False - it was a No.1 for The Rubettes in 1974.

HAPPY BIRTHDAY No.8

Can you identify these musicians?

1. Singer born in Stafford, England on 23 July 1973.

2. Singer and pianist born in Saginaw, USA on 13 May 1950.

3. Singer and actor born in Malvern, Victoria, Australia on 1 June 1968.

4. Drummer born in Dudley, England on 15 July 1966.

5. Singer and guitarist born in Akron, Ohio, USA on 7 September 1951.

6. Singer born in Oldham, England on 27 January 1972.

7. Rapper born in Accra, Ghana on 14 September 1986.

8. Drummer and singer born in Gilmer, Texas, USA on 22 July 1947.

9. Singer born in Prestatyn, Wales on 25 February 1959.

10. Singer born in Blackpool, England on 2 February 1942.

11. Singer and actress born in Franklin, Tennessee, USA on 23 November 1992.

12. DJ and musician born in Rotterdam, Netherlands on 1 February 1995.

13. Singer and guitarist born in Glasgow, Scotland on 4 March 1979.

14. Singer born in Dublin, Ireland on 16 October 1991.

15. Singer born in Detroit, USA on 26 March 1944.

16. Singer and TV star born in Newcastle upon Tyne, England on 30 June 1983.

17. Drummer born in Kilmarnock, Scotland on 1 May 1956.

18. Guitarist born in Corning, New York, USA on 26 April 1938.

19. Singer born in Croydon, England on 10 October 1959.

20. Singer born in Safed, Palestine on 13 June 1941.

HAPPY BIRTHDAY No.8

Answers

1. Fran Healy.
2. Stevie Wonder.
3. Jason Donovan.
4. Jason Bonham.
5. Chrissie Hynde.
6. Mark Owen.
7. Tinchy Stryder.
8. Don Henley.
9. Mike Peters.
10. Graham Nash.
11. Miley Cyrus.
12. Oliver Heldens.
13. John Fratelli.
14. John Grimes ..... as was Edward Grimes also!
15. Diana Ross.
16. Cheryl (Tweedy).
17. Mike Ogletree.
18. Duane Eddy.
19. Kirsty MacColl.
20. Esther Ofarim.

WHO ARE YOU? No.15

Which name is missing from these song titles?

1. _____ bites the worm (Bluetones)
2. Hello _____ (Amen Corner)
3. _____ (Mark Owen)
4. The day I met _____ (Cliff Richard)
5. _____ come home (Fine Young Canibals)
6. _____ (Bachelors)
7. Ms _____ (The Tymes)
8. _____ come lately (Brian Hyland)
9. _____ (Supergrass)
10. Bull in the _____ (Sonic Youth)
11. ____ in the box (Clodagh Rodgers)
12. _____ baby (Helen Reddy)
13. _____ _____ (Undertones)
14. Lady _____ (Beach Boys)
15. _____ ____ (Hollies)
16. ____ Maclennane (Pogues)
17. Which way you going _____ ? (Poppy Family)
18. _____ ain't dead (Scouting for Girls)
19. Who's _____ ? (Busted)
20. _____ (Robbie Williams)

WHO ARE YOU? No.15

Answers

1. Solomon.
2. Susie.
3. Clementine.
4. Marie.
5. Johnny.
6. Diane ..... or Marie.
7. Grace.
8. Ginny.
9. Lenny.
10. Heather.
11. Jack.
12. Angie.
13. Jimmy, Jimmy.
14. Lynda.
15. Carrie Anne.
16. Sally.
17. Billy.
18. Elvis.
19. David.
20. Grace.

THE NAME GAME No.16

By what names are the following better known:

1. Steven Kapur.
2. Lynsey Monckton Rubin.
3. Prakazrel Samuel Michel.
4. Dorothy Sherratt.
5. Jacques Pepino.
6. Michael Hubert Bourne.
7. James Sammon.
8. Nancy Richardson.
9. Damon Michael Gough.
10. Lugee Alfredo Giovanni Sacco.
11. Peter Anthony Robinson.
12. Shayaa Bin Abraham - Joseph.
13. Gabriele Susanne Kerner.
14. Maurice James Christopher Cole.
15. Gerhard Friedle.
16. Matthew Shafer.
17. Hugh Anthony Cregg.
18. Heidi Stern.
19. Iyael Iyases Tafari Constable.
20. Terrence Charles White.

THE NAME GAME No.16

Answers

1. Apache Indian.
2. Lynsey de Paul.
3. Pras.
4. Natasha (and that's her middle name).
5. David Christie.
6. Mike Berry.
7. Pianoman.
8. Taja Sevelle.
9. Badly Drawn Boy.
10. Lou Christie.
11 Marilyn.
12. 21 Savage.
13. Nena.
14. Kenny Everett.
15. DJ Otzi.
16. Uncle Kracker.
17. Huey Lewis.
18. Jennifer Rush.
19. Glamma Kid.
20. Snowy White

BLANK SPACE No.16

Fill in the blanks to reveal bands that have had chart hits:

1. S _ S _ E _ S   _ F   _ E _ C _
2. B _ Y   _ I _ Y   _ O _ L _ R _
3. H _ O _ I _   A _ D   _ H _   B _ O _ F _ S _
4. S _ L _ A _ S   _ F   _ I _ G
5. F _ V _   S _ A _
6. M _ G _ T _   L _ M _ N   _ R _ P _
7. T _ L _   T _ L _
8. L _ D _ S _ I _ H   _ L _ C _   M _ M _ A _ O
9. B _ D   _ A _ N _ R _
10. S _ E _ P   _ N   _ R _ G _
11. T _ D _   T _ R _ Y   _ R _ J _ C _
12. E _ E _ T _ O _ I _
13. E _ E _ T _ I _   S _ X
14. W _ I _ E   _ L _ I _ S
15. P _ A _ E _ O
16. N _ D _   A _ O _ I _   D _ S _ B _ N
17. B _ R _ O _   K _ I _ H _ S
18. T _ R _ N   _ R _ K _ S
19. C _ I _ A   _ R _ S _ S
20. S _ E _ R   _ L _ G _ N _ E

BLANK SPACE No.16

ANSWERS

1. Sisters of Mercy.
2. Bay City Rollers.
3. Hootie and the Blowfish.
4. Sultans of Ping.
5. Five Star.
6. Mighty Lemon Drops.
7. Talk Talk.
8. Ladysmith Black Mambazo.
9. Bad Manners.
10. Sheep on Drugs.
11. Todd Terry Project.
12. Electronic.
13. Electric Six.
14. White Plains.
15. Placebo.
16. Ned's Atomic Dustbin.
17. Barron Knights.
18. Turin Brakes.
19. China Crisis.
20. Sheer Elegance.

LUCKY NUMBER No.8

Which cardinal or ordinal numbers are missing from these song titles?

1   Swords of a _____ men (Tenpole Tudor)
2   _____ words (Cheryl Cole with Will.i.am)
3   _____ dollar bill (Whitney Houston)
4   _____ with a bullet (Pete Wingfield)
5   Kernkraft _____ (Zombie Nation)
6   _____ (Britney Spears)
7   Put your hands up _____ Detroit (Fedde Le Grand)
8   _____ years time (Noah and the Whale)
9   _____ century Christmas (Cliff Richard)
10 _____ questions (50 Cent with Nate Dogg)
11 Room on the _____ floor (McFly)
12 Be the _____ (Dua Lipa)
13 _____ : _____ (The Strokes)
14 Star _____ (Fat Boy Slim)
15 Mambo No. _____ (Lou Bega)
16 Positively _____ Street (Bob Dylan)
17 Car _____ (Driver 67)
18 _____ % (Sonic Youth)
19 _____ century boy (T Rex)
20 _____ seconds (So Solid Crew)

LUCKY NUMBER No.8

Answers

1   Thousand.
2   Three.
3   Million.
4   Eighteen.
5   Four hundred.
6   Three.
7   Four.
8   Five.
9   Twenty first.
10 Twenty one.
11 Third.
12 One.
13 Twelve / Fifty one.
14 Sixty nine.
15 Five.
16 Fourth.
17 Sixty seven.
18 One hundred.
19 Twentieth.
20 Twenty one.

TWO OF US No.7

Can you complete the names of these duos?

1. Diana Brown and ?
2. Keith 'N' ?
3. DJ Misjah and ?
4. Lester Flatt and ?
5. Bump and ?
6. Vinylgroover and ?
7. England Dan and ?
8. Rae and ?
9. Karen Boddington and ?
10. Phil Oakley and ?
11. Trina and ?
12. Seiko and ?
13. Millican and ?
14. Ping Ping and ?
15. Chad and ?
16. Les Paul and ?
17. Liz Kershaw and ?
18. Wendy and ?
19. Ollie and ?
20. John Parish and ?

TWO OF US No.7

Answers

1. Barrie K Sharpe.
2. Shane (Duffy and Lynch).
3. DJ Tim.
4. Earl Scruggs.
5. Flex.
6. The Red Hed.
7. John Ford Coley.
8. Christian.
9. Mark Williams.
10. Giorgio Moroder.
11. Tamara (the Powell sisters).
12. Donnie Wahlberg.
13. Nesbit.
14. Al Verlane.
15. Jeremy (Stuart and Clyde).
16. Mary Ford.
17. Bruno Brookes.
18. Lisa (Melvion and Coleman - aka Girl Bros).
19. Jerry (Brown and Knight).
20. Polly Jean Harvey.

WORDS No.16

Can you identify these famous songs from their opening lyrics:

1. She ain't got no money, her clothes are kinda funny, her hair is kinda wild ....

2. Right now, I'm in a state of mind I wanna be in like all the time ....

3. Marvin, he was a friend of mine and he could sing a song. His heart in every line ....

4. You're everywhere and nowhere baby, that's where you're at ....

5. Yeah, as a shorty playing in the front yard of the crib, fell down and bumped ...

6. Call you up in the middle of the night, like a firefly without a light ...

7. Oh, Let's go. Steve walks warily down the street, with the brim pulled way down low. Ain't no sound .....

8. Get out from that kitchen and rattle those pots and pans. Get out from that kitchen .....

9. Take a breath, take it deep. Calm yourself he says to me. If you play, you play ....

10. Baby, we can talk all night, but that ain't gettin us nowhere. I told you everything ....

11. Is it wrong to want to live on your own? No, it's not wrong, but I must know ....

12. I'd like to play a game that is so much fun, and it's not so very hard to do ....

13. Every butterfly I get belongs to you. You don't believe me, but it's true .....

14. Loving you isn't the right thing to do. How can I ever change things that I feel? ...

15. Go on and close the curtains 'cause all we need is candlelight. You and me ...

16. Ah, click click. Ah, click click. I've been checking you up, I've been tracking ....

17. If I had one chance to live my life again, I wouldn't make no changes .....

18. Next time you're found with your chin on the ground. There's a lot to be learned ....

19. So, we waved our hands as we marched along, and the people smiled as we sang ....

20. Tell me a story where we all change, and we'd live our lives together and not enstranged .....

WORDS No.16

Answers

1. Love grows (where my Rosemary goes) (Edison Lighthouse).
2. No tears left to cry (Ariana Grande).
3. Nightshift (Commodores).
4. Hi ho silver lining (Jeff Beck).
5. Gimme some more (Busta Rhymes).
6. Runaway train (Soul Asylum).
7. Another one bites the dust (Queen).
8. Shake rattle and roll (Bill Haley).
9. Russian roulette (Rihanna).
10. Two out of three ain't bad (Meat Loaf).
11. Sheila take a bow (Smiths).
12. Simon says (1910 Fruitgum Company).
13. All I am (Jess Glynne).
14. Go your own way (Fleetwood Mac).
15. Save tonight (Eagle Eye Cherry).
16. My camera never lies (Bucks Fizz).
17. Real girl (Mutya Buena).
18. High hopes (Frank Sinatra).
19. Banner man (Blue Mink).
20. No regrets (Robbie Williams).

THERE'S A PLACE No.10

Which place name is missing from these song titles?

1   _ _ _ _ _ (Chainsmokers)

2   This is _ _ _ _ _ _ _ ? (The Clash)

3   _ _ _ _ _ _ _ song (Keane)

4   New _ _ _ _ _ _ _ _ (Elvis Costello)

5   _ _ _ _ _ melody (Helmut Zacharius)

6   Big in _ _ _ _ _ (Alphaville)

7   Drowning in _ _ _ _ _ _ (Mobiles)

8   _ _ _ _ _ _ (Camila Cabello with Young Thug)

9   _ _ _ _ _ _ _ _ (Fat Les 2000)

10 The return of the _ _ _ _ _ _ _ _ _ 7 (Madness)

11 Dani _ _ _ _ _ _ _ _ _ _ (Red Hot Chilli Peppers)

12 _ _ _ _ _ _ bridge (Fergie)

13 Put your hands up 4 _ _ _ _ _ _ _ (Fedde Le Grand)

14 Leaving _ _ _ _ _ _ _ (REM)

15 Diamonds from _ _ _ _ _ _ _ _ _ _ _ (Kanye West)

16 A song about the boys from _ _ _ _ _ _ _ _ _ (Silver Convention)

17 Leaving _ _ _ _ _ _ _ _ (Sheryl Crow)

18 Let the boss kick in _ _ _ _ _ girl (Chuckie & LMFAO)

19 Under the bridges of _ _ _ _ _ (Dean Martin)

20 _ _ _ _ _ _ _ _ _ (Manic Street Preachers)

THERE'S A PLACE No.10

Answers

1   Paris.
2   England.
3   Hamburg.
4   Amsterdam.
5   Tokyo.
6   Japan.
7   Berlin.
8   Havana.
9   Jerusalem.
10 Las Palmas.
11 California.
12 London.
13 Detroit.
14 New York.
15 Sierra Leone.
16 Liverpool.
17 Las Vegas.
18 Miami.
19 Paris.
20 Australia.

ANY COLOUR YOU LIKE No.6

Which colour is missing from these song titles?

1   _____ guitar (Justin Hayward and John Lodge)

2   Little _____ berry (Roy Castle)

3   _____ burning heart (Keane)

4   _____ pills (DIZ)

5   _____ (Daniel Merriweather)

6   Goodbye _____ brick road (Elton John)

7   Misty _____ (Dorothy Moore)

8   _____ star (Four Seasons)

9   _____ and _____ (Greyhound)

10   Pretty _____ eyes (Ultrabeat)

11   _____ (Hole)

12   Soldier _____ (Buffy Sainte-Marie)

13   Fields of _____ (Sting)

14   Behind _____ eyes (Who)

15   Hi ho _____ (Jim Diamond)

16   _____ (Moloko)

17   _____ moon (Nick Drake)

18   _____ hole sun (Soundgarden)

19   _____ and clover (Tommy James)

20   Bullet in the _____ sky (U2)

ANY COLOUR YOU LIKE No.6

Answers

1   Blue.
2   White.
3   Black.
4   Purple.
5   Red.
6   Yellow.
7   Blue.
8   Silver.
9   Black, white.
10 Green.
11 Violet.
12 Blue.
13 Gold.
14 Blue.
15 Silver.
16 Indigo.
17 Pink.
18 Black.
19 Crimson.
20 Blue.

EMPTY SPACES No.17

Fill in the blanks to reveal musicians who have had chart hits:

1. D _ M _ E _   R _ C _
2. G _ O _ G _ E   _ A _ E
3. J _ A _   B _ E _
4. T _ N _ T _   T _ K _ R _ M
5. A _ E _ A _ D _ A   _ T _ N
6. H _ R _ I _ A _ E   _ M _ T _
7. J _ S _ N   _ E _ U _ O
8. A _ E _ H _   F _ A _ K _ I _
9. C _ T   _ T _ V _ N _
10. T _ J _   _ E _ E _ L _
11. F _ E _ A   _ I _ I _ G _
12. E _ M _ N _   H _ C _ R _ D _ E
13. J _ H _   S _ C _ D _
14. M _ R _ O _   R _ U _ E _ T _
15. R _ C _ E _   S _ E _ E _ S
16. D _ M _ S   _ O _ S _ O _
17. L _ C _ E   _ I _ V _ S
18 G _ R _ Y   _ A _ F _ R _ Y
19. S _ I _ L _ Y   _ A _ S _ Y
20. R _ Y   _ R _ I _ O _

EMPTY SPACES No.17

ANSWERS

1. Damien Rice.
2. Georgie Fame.
3. Joan Baez.
4. Tanita Tikaram.
5. Alexandra Stan.
6. Hurricane Smith.
7. Jason Derulo.
8. Aretha Franklin.
9. Cat Stevens.
10. Taja Sevelle.
11. Freya Ridings.
12. Edmund Hockridge.
13. John Secada.
14. Marlon Roudette.
15. Rachel Stevens.
16. Demis Roussos.
17. Lucie Silvas.
18. Gerry Rafferty.
19. Shirley Bassey.
20. Roy Orbison.

MIX IT UP No.9

Can you unravel the anagrams to identify these hit making bands?

1. HE SKIPS TIN KING
2. MATES
3. NOW STORM BOAT
4. FRY TIMES SCORES
5. EXIT ON RANGE
6. SECRET PAINTER MARCHES
7. MARKET NOW
8. WET HANKIES
9. BRAND NAMES
10. MILDER SPY
11. MEN COSH BOY
12. ROCKS IN SHAME
13. I TEXT MILL
14. TO ECHO AT LOCH
15. ONCE SURE COOL CANE
16. TAIL SANG
17. HARMS THE MINERS
18. RUM TIN DEAL
19. HUEY OF BRENT
20. TOES CARRY BILLY

MIX IT UP No.9

Answers

1. KISSING THE PINK
2. STEAM
3. BOOMTOWN RATS
4. SISTERS OF MERCY
5. GENERATION X
6. MANIC STREET PREACHERS
7. MEN AT WORK
8. WHITESNAKE
9. BAD MANNERS
10. SIMPLY RED
11. HONEYCOMBS
12. CHAINSMOKERS
13. LITTLE MIX
14. HOT CHOCOLATE
15. OCEAN COLOUR SCENE
16. GALANTIS
17. HERMAN'S HERMITS
18. RUDIMENTAL
19. FUN BOY THREE
20. BAY CITY ROLLERS

COMMON PEOPLE No.6

What do the following have in common?

1. Poor little fool, It's up to you, Just a little too much, Young world, I got a feeling.

2. Three lions, Spaceman, A different beat, Firestarter, Setting sun.

3. Accelerate, Come fly with me, Revelation, The long road back, Natural.

4. Trevor Horn, Paul Morley, Anne Dudley, Gary Langan, Lol Creme.

5. Shirley Manson, Craig Reid, David Paton, Finley Quaye, Les McKeown.

6. Eight by ten, Brokenhearted, Let me cry on your shoulder, Promises, Pianissimo.

7. Paloma Faith, James Arthur, Geri Halliwell, Pixie Lott, Roger Daltrey.

8. Big love, Simplified, Men and women, Love and the Russian winter, Picture book.

9. Dido, Annie Lennox, Shane McGowan, Kenny Everett, Alannah Miles.

10. Sally Graham, Peter Doyle, Paul Layton, Kathy Ann Rae, Peter Oliver.

11. She loves you, Mull of Kintyre, Do they know it's Christmas?, Candle in the wind, Anything is possible.

12. Neil Finn, John Rowles, Kiri Te Kanawa, Hayley Westenra, Daniel Beddingfield.

13. Ivy League, Edison Lighthouse, Brotherhood of Man, Flower Pot Men, White Plains.

14. Sing a favourite song, Portrait, Tribute to the crooners, Just for you, With love.

15. Congratulations, Surround yourself (with sorrow), Shang-a-lang, Puppet on a string, Forever and ever.

16. Ricky Valance, David Zowie, Althea and Donna, Lena Martell, Norman Greenbaum.

17. Dennis Taylor, Willie Thorne, Terry Griffiths, Tony Meo, Steve Davis.

18. Lorraine, Doris, Steadman, Denise, Delroy.

19. Bloody Mary, Some enchanted evening, Happy talk, There is nothing like a dame, Younger than springtime.

20. Everything changes, Let me be your fantasy, Doop, Saturday night, Inside.

COMMON PEOPLE No.6

ANSWERS

1. They were all hit singles by Ricky Nelson.
2. They all topped the singles chart in 1996.
3. They are all albums by Peter Andre.
4. They were all members of the 'Art of Noise'.
5. They were all born in Edinburgh.
6. They were all hit singles by Ken Dodd.
7. They were all 'Artists for Grenfell'.
8. They are all hit albums by Simply Red.
9. They were all born on Christmas Day.
10. They were all members of The New Seekers.
11. They were the top selling singles of the decade - 60's to 00's.
12. They were all born in New Zealand.
13. Tony Burrows was a singer with all of them.
14. They are all hit albums by Des O'Connor.
15. They were all written by Bill Martin and Phil Coulter.
16. They all reached No.1 with their one and only hit single.
17. They were 'The Matchroom Mob' - the backing singers for Chas and Dave on their hit 'Snooker loopy'.
18. They are the Pearson siblings who make up Five Star.
19. They are all songs from South Pacific.
20. They were all No.1 hits from 1994.

THE NAME GAME No.17

By what names are the following better known:

1. John Paul Larkin.
2. Yvonne Stevens.
3. Neville Williams.
4. Adam Paul Tinley.
5. Beatrice Melba Hill.
6. Louis Sharpe.
7. Louis Ferdinand Busch.
8. Manuela Barbara Kamosi.
9. David Keith Arratoon.
10. Cecil Bustamente Campbell.
11. Vivian Vanessa Kubrick.
12. Jeanne-Paule Marie Deckers.
13. O'Shae Jackson.
14. Lance Taylor.
15. Patricia Louise Holt.
16. William Bruce Rose Jnr.
17. Samuel Frankland Falson.
18. Mark McLachlan.
19. Artis Leon Ivey Jnr.
20. Michael Barratt.

THE NAME GAME No.17

Answers

1. Scatman John.
2. Taka Boom.
3. Gary Miller.
4. Adamski (aka Adam Sky and Sony Eriksson).
5. Melba Moore.
6. K7 (aka Kayel).
7. Joe 'Fingers' Carr (aka Lou Busch).
8. Ya Kid K.
9. David Jordan.
10. Prince Buster.
11. Abigail Mead.
12. The Singing Nun (aka Soeur Sourire and Luc Dominique).
13. Ice Cube.
14. Afrika Bambaataa.
15. Patti Labelle.
16. Axl Rose.
17. Sam Sparro.
18. Marti Pellow.
19. Coolio.
20. Shakin' Stevens.

OTHER BOOKS BY THIS AUTHOR:

SCORE!: The unusual book of football trivia

The Bottles: Scotland's favourite pop group

Molvie's Children

Some Silly Safety Stories

© Brian Whyte 2019

Printed in Great Britain
by Amazon